LIFE IN ANGLO-SAXON ENGLAND

David the harpist and accompanying musicians
BM Cotton MS Vespasian A I. f. 3ov.

Life in
ANGLO-SAXON
ENGLAND

R. I. PAGE

English Life Series
EDITED BY PETER QUENNELL

LONDON: B. T. Batsford Ltd
NEW YORK: G. P. Putnam's Sons

To E.L.P. and the memory of R.H.P.

First published 1970
© R. I. Page, 1970
7134 4161 8

Printed and bound in Great Britain by
Jarrold & Sons Ltd, Norwich and London
for the publishers
B. T. BATSFORD LTD
4 Fitzhardinge Street, London W.1
G. P. PUTNAM'S SONS
200 Madison Avenue, New York, NY 10016

Preface

Anglo-Saxon England lasted for six centuries, the time that separates Harold, last of their kings, from Charles II, or Chaucer and Edward III from ourselves. Change was much slower in the early Middle Ages than it is today, yet over 600 years there was change. Everyday life in the mid fifth century, when the Anglo-Saxons were pagan invaders fighting Christian defenders, was different from that at the end of the tenth, when they were Christian defenders fighting pagan invaders. Nor was everyday life the same over the whole country. A Northumbrian peasant in the depths of the Yorkshire dales lived differently from a worker on a royal estate in Wessex. Any book on Anglo-Saxon daily life must be very much a simplification, picking out salient features of the time and encouraging the reader to further investigation by showing the range of sources, archaeological and written, literary, linguistic and historical, Latin and vernacular, available to us. This is all I have attempted. Specialists in the various fields may feel that my treatment of their subjects is cavalier—for example, the archaeologist will remark that, in my section on houses, I have avoided refinements of dating and the development of building techniques, while the numismatist may regret that I have not stressed economic aspects of the administrative system which the later Anglo-Saxon kings commanded. I can only plead lack of space.

In several fields our knowledge of Anglo-Saxon England is rapidly increasing. To take two examples: it is only in comparatively recent years that scholars have realised the light that numismatic studies can cast on Anglo-Saxon historical and social conditions; the many archaeologists digging settlement, industrial and ecclesiastical sites are revolutionising our knowledge of technical processes and building methods. The general social historian can hope only to be as up to date as possible in fields like these, knowing that some of his statements may quickly be outmoded.

On the whole I have avoided quoting forms in Old English, the tongue spoken by the Anglo-Saxons. Occasionally I have had to use words from that language, and then I have kept the form of the original except for using *th* rather than the obsolete symbol þ, called *thorn* (though *thorn* appears in my account of the runic amulet rings where I want to retain the same number of letters as the inscriptions). I give personal names of well-known historical figures in their familiar forms—it would be absurd to call Alfred the Great *Ælfred*, or Edward the Confessor *Eadward*—but for less famous people I have used name-forms approaching the original. My spelling is thus not always consistent, but luckily neither was that of the Anglo-Saxons.

I cannot thank by name everyone who has helped me write this book, for it derives from the work of the last 15 years, during which time people of many disciplines, art historians, numismatists, archaeologists, historians, linguists and literary scholars, have answered my enquiries. Four scholars I must thank specifically for their assistance. Professor Dorothy Whitelock read through the book in draft form, and from her encyclopaedic knowledge of the period gave me a great deal of invaluable advice. Mr D. M. Wilson helped me notably in the archaeological sections, and suggested much of the material I use there. Professor Bruce Dickins and Dr B. Hope-Taylor have read parts of my text, which has profited from their acute criticisms. Finally, I must thank my wife and children for showing their customary forbearance while I was engaged in this work.

R. I. PAGE

Contents

Acknowledgment

The author and publishers wish to thank the following for permission to reproduce the illustrations appearing in this book: Aerofilms and Aero Pictorial Ltd for page 119; the *Archaeological Journal* for page 147; Hallam Ashley, F.R.P.S., for page 164; the Ashmolean Museum, Oxford, for page 55; Museum of Archaeology and Ethnology, Cambridge, for pages 72, 75; the Bodleian Library, Oxford, for pages 20, 77, 82, 83, 84, 85, 105, 123; the Trustees of the British Museum for the frontispiece and pages 2, 5, 6, 7, 9, 19, 21, 22, 23, 29, 30, 31, 34, 40, 42, 43, 46, 47, 48, 49, 51, 52, 67, 68, 69, 77, 78, 79, 81, 83 (top), 86, 89, 90, 91, 94, 95, 96, 99, 100, 104, 105, 110, 111, 112, 121, 124, 125, 126, 128, 129, 131, 132, 133, 152, 153, 156, 163, 166, 167, 168, 169 (both), 170; the Master and Fellows of Corpus Christi College, Cambridge, for pages 38, 63, 118, 159; the Courtauld Institute for page 49; the Dean and Chapter of Durham for pages 76 and 120; Photo-Giraudon, Paris, for page 51 (top); *Illustrated London News* for page 140; A. F. Kersting, F.R.P.S., for pages 87, 115, 116; the City of Liverpool Museum for page 24; *Medieval Archaeology* for page 146; Phaidon Press Ltd for pages 4, 8, 10–11, 50, 51 (bottom), 58, 103, 139, 143, 165, 167; Dr J. K. St Joseph for pages 13, 17, 106, 142; the City of Sheffield Museum for page 31; the Science Museum for page 16; Alan Sorrell for page 140; the Master and Fellows of Trinity College, Cambridge, for page 35; the Ministry of Public Buildings and Works (Crown copyright reserved) for pages 3, 14; Riks antikvariè ämbetet, Stockholm, for page 12.

The Illustrations

I

The Violent Tenor of Life

According to tradition the Anglo-Saxons reached England in the first half of the fifth century. Their political power was destroyed in the second half of the eleventh. In the six centuries which separate these events, they created their arts, handicrafts, literature, forms of government, society and agricultural and mercantile activity amid the turmoils typical of the early Middle Ages. The settlement of England was violent. The *Anglo-Saxon Chronicle* tells of the struggle between Saxon and Briton in the south and west of the country in the fifth and sixth centuries, and other sources describe the fluctuating fortunes of war and the fierce resistance which the Britons offered at various times and places. Even after the settlement had established the pattern of Anglo-Saxon occupation, strife did not cease, for the small early Anglo-Saxon kingdoms were constantly clashing with one another and with the remaining Celtic peoples. In 597 Ceolwulf became king of Wessex, and 'continually fought . . . against the Angles, or against the Welsh, or against the Picts, or against the Scots'. In 603 Aethelfrith of Northumbria broke the Celts of western Scotland at *Degsastan*, but in the battle lost his brother Theobald with all his bodyguard. In 626 Edwin of Northumbria was treacherously attacked by an assassin sent by Cwichelm of Wessex, and in revenge invaded that kingdom and 'killed five kings there and a great number of people'. Edwin, and his son Osfrith with him, died in battle at the hands of the British leader Cadwallon and Penda of Mercia, who then devastated Northumbria. Penda subsequently killed Edwin's other son Eanfrith, and king Oswald of Northumbria, and was in turn slain by Oswiu, Oswald's brother and successor. In 686

Armed men attack a house: an archer defends it

Ceadwalla of Wessex annexed the Isle of Wight and massacred its inhabitants. At about the same time Guthlac, of the royal house of Mercia, gathered a band of warriors from various races, and 'devastated the towns and manors of his foes, their villages and fortresses with fire and the sword', though, as a sign of the divine grace which was to lead him to sainthood, 'he would return to the owners a third part of the treasure collected'.

Within the Anglo-Saxon kingdoms themselves strife was intermittent, often between the great nobles or between rival claimants to the throne. Usually our sources give us only the bare bones of the story, as in the cases of the burning of the ealdorman Beorn by the high-reeves of Northumbria in 780, the conflict between Osred and Aethelred for the Northumbrian kingship which ended with the killing of Osred in 792 and the death of Aethelred, slain by his own people four years later, and—though here we have rather more detail—the murder of king Edward to allow the accession of his brother Aethelred in 978. Occasionally we have fuller information and a clearer picture of political struggle. In 786 Cynewulf, king of Wessex, was trapped in his mistress's house by a rival prince, Cyneheard, and was cut down with nearly all the small bodyguard he had brought with him. When the rest of Cynewulf's retainers heard of the killing, they surrounded and stormed the homestead, and in their turn slaughtered Cyneheard and 84 of his supporters. A circumstantial report is preserved in the *Chronicle*, perhaps because it had become a popular tale among the Anglo-Saxons. A piece of brutality some 250 years later moved the compiler of

2

the *Chronicle* to poetic composition. In the struggle for power following the death of the mighty king Cnut, earl Godwine seized prince Alfred, who was then blinded and confined to the monastery of Ely. His followers Godwine drove into flight

> *and some he killed in various ways,*
> *Some of them were sold for cash, some cruelly slaughtered,*
> *Some of them were fettered, some blinded,*
> *Some were mutilated, some scalped.*
> *No more dreadful deed has been done in this land*
> *Since the Danes came and took peace at our hands.*

From the late eighth century onwards there was a further source of violence in the country, the Vikings. About the year 790 three ships, described as Norwegian, came to the south coast near Dorchester. The king's reeve thought the crews were foreign merchants and tried to control them according to law. They killed him. The closing years of the eighth century saw piratical attacks on the coastal monasteries of Lindisfarne and Jarrow, and during the ninth there was a series of determined

A stone from Lindisfarne, showing a file of fighting men, perhaps Vikings

3

and ferocious onslaughts which resulted in the Scandinavian settlement of the north and east, and an embattled Wessex fighting off the invader. The Vikings returned in the late years of the tenth century, assaulting England with renewed ferocity under leaders with more consciously imperialist aims, and remained a threat until after the Norman Conquest. The *Chronicle* writers gave the Vikings a bad press, and they clearly deserved it. Their own surviving literature—the odes the court poets wrote in praise of their kings and the inscriptions of their memorial stones—shows a delight in bloodthirsty action, so it is not surprising to read in the *Chronicle* for 994 of the army of the kings Olaf and Swein 'doing as much damage as any host could do in burning, harrying, and slaughter, both along the coast and in Essex, Kent, Sussex, and Hampshire', or of Cnut's army of 1016, which 'turned into Warwickshire . . . and harried and burned and killed all they came upon'. Certainly the Vikings acted like savages on occasion, as in 1012 when, in a drunken frenzy, they brutally murdered the archbishop Aelfheah whom they were holding to ransom, by pelting him with bones and the heads of cattle.

I do not suggest that the history of Anglo-Saxon England is one of battle and sudden death only, or that during the six centuries of Anglo-Saxon occupation England was in a state of anarchy. The country was sometimes—for a medieval land—secure, law-abiding and well administered. For quite long periods of time there was little organised warfare. Bede boasts that the reign of Edwin of Northumbria was so peaceful that a woman carrying a new-born babe could walk across the island from sea to sea without danger of molestation, and in a verse passage in the *Chronicle* on the death of Edgar in 975, the writer comments: 'No fleet was so proud, nor host so strong that it could prey on England while that noble king held the throne.'

A house is burnt down: mother and child escape

Battle and sudden death

But even at these times the Anglo-Saxon lived in closer contact with violence than the average Englishman of today. The blood-feud was a feature of social behaviour and the royal legal codes which supplemented customary law recognised it and indeed legislated for it. The law itself was violent, though a trespasser would often avoid its severer penalties by paying a fine if he could afford it. The various extant codes—which differ a lot from each other—prescribe the death penalty for a variety of offenders; thieves and those who harboured, supported or avenged them, traitors, witches and wizards who killed by their arts, incendiaries, absconding slaves, those who protected outlaws, and so on. Methods of execution included hanging, beheading, stoning, burning, drowning and breaking the neck. Among lesser penalties were mutilations such as cutting off hands, feet, nose, ears, upper lip or tongue, blinding, castration and scalping, as well as branding and scourging. Humane clerics preferred such punishments, for they gave the sinner time to

5

'One man must ride on the broad gallows'

repent. And the law's rigour was not hidden from men. A poem called *The Fates of Men* describes thus the exposure of the hanged body upon the gibbet. 'One man must ride on the broad gallows, swing in death until the casket of his soul, his bleeding corpse, is torn to shreds as the dark-coated raven steals his eyes, rends the dead creature. His hands cannot ward off the attack of the flying destroyer, but, without feeling or hope of life, he endures his fate, pale upon the gibbet.' The law often used brutal methods of investigation, for a defendant could sometimes only clear himself by undergoing the ordeal— by bearing a weight of hot iron for three or nine feet, or plucking a stone from a vessel of boiling water. And the law often encouraged brutality in the apprehension of suspects or culprits. One who tried to escape or to defend himself could be cut down, however small the offence and however young the offender. A man could attack with legal impunity another whom he caught in fornication with his wife, mother, daughter or sister. A stranger who travelled off the recognised way and who neither shouted nor blew a horn to announce his presence could be assumed to be a thief and killed out of hand.

Side by side with the violence of man was the violence of a nature over which man had little control. Particularly terrible was famine, and its companions murrain and plague, such as harried England in the early years of Edward the Confessor's reign. In 1042 tempests damaged the crops, and storm and plague killed the cattle. In 1044 there was famine, with corn 'dearer than anyone remembered it, so that a sester of wheat cost 60 pence and more'—worse even than the year of dearth, 1039, when it had reached only 55. 1046–7 was a fearful winter, with the death of birds and fish from cold and starvation. The accompanying pestilence which struck the country lasted into 1048, while in 1054 the cattle died of murrain. Visitations like

6

these could destroy the small communities of Anglo-Saxon England. In 830, Canterbury tradition tells, the town was so stricken with disease that in Christ Church only five monks survived. Certainly at this date there is confusion in the succession of archbishops which suggests that the Canterbury community had become quite disorganised. About 1014 archbishop Wulfstan of York, who looked on the black side of things and saw in the troubles of his times signs of the approaching dissolution of the world, listed England's miseries. Apart from the perennial worries, high taxation and bad weather, they were 'devastation and famine, burning and bloodshed . . . theft and killing, plague and pestilence, murrain and disease, envy, hatred and rapine'. The cruelty of man and the cruelty of nature were alike seen as God's punishment of an impious people.

Under these conditions it is not surprising that the life of Anglo-Saxon man, often poor, nasty and brutish, was often also short. *The Fates of Men* catalogues the deaths a man may die. The list compares interestingly with its modern equivalent, for we have suppressed many of its dangers and replaced them by different, but equally ferocious, ones. The Anglo-Saxon was threatened by attack by the wolf, hunger, storm, feud and war, a tumble from a tree presumably while at work, hanging, fire and the drunken brawl. The alternative—and it is represented as a triumphant one—is to live till old age, honoured and wealthy. Of course we must not underestimate the Anglo-Saxon's expectation of life, Many survived long. Ceolnoth occupied the see of Canterbury for 36 years, while Ealhstan was bishop of Sherborne for 43 and Waerfrith bishop of Worcester for 42, so all three must have reached a respectable age. Yet these were probably exceptional. I quote in contrast the ages at

More battle and sudden death

death of the later kings of Wessex and of England, insofar as we know them. Alfred the Great was 50 when he died; Edmund, murdered, 25; Edgar 32; Edward, also murdered, about 17. Aethelred the Unready died at about 47, Cnut the Great at about 40, Hardacnut in his 20s. Edward the Confessor in his early 60s, while Harold, last of the Anglo-Saxon kings, was killed at Hastings in his mid 40s. The evidence of the Anglo-Saxon cemeteries has not been properly assessed, but a few examples are revealing. At Camerton, Somerset, which may have been a plague cemetery of the seventh century, 115 bodies were found, 16 of them of children and 24 of infants. Few were of people over 40, and many of them suggest undernourishment. The statistics of two smaller cemeteries dug recently are more precise. The seventh-century cemetery at Holborough, Kent, contained 32 bodies, and there were also two graves which had probably contained infants. Twenty-three bodies were of under 30s, eight between 30 and 45, only one above 45. From Little Eriswell, Suffolk, a sixth-century cemetery of a community of

Death of Edward the Confessor

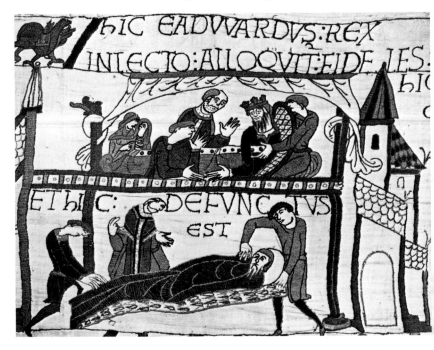

the middle social range, 26 bodies were examined. Only four were of people over 35, and none of them lived beyond 50. Fourteen died between 20 and 35, three in adolescence and five as children.

A dead man goes to his grave

High infant and child mortality, frequent attacks of pestilence, deaths from weakness, hunger and infection, physical oppression and violence from personal or political enemies, all these must have been commonplaces of Anglo-Saxon existence; life evidently transitory and subject to sudden change. In much of the vernacular poetry, which survives from the later period, critics have found a strong strain of melancholy, of regret at life's passing, of lament for the decay of worldly splendour and for the loss of friends and kin. Of course, such themes have been popular in many ages; a contempt for earthly things and a recognition of the vanity of human wishes springs naturally from the strongly Christian civilisation of Anglo-Saxon England. Yet this poetry, often quite sophisticated, reflects, too, the physical conditions of Anglo-Saxon life, so often nasty, brutish and short. For example, the poem called (in modern times) *The Ruin* is a meditation upon a deserted Roman city, apparently Bath, once great, now fallen from high estate:

> *Bright were its palaces, its many bathing-halls,*
> *Its wealth of tall pinnacles, its tumult of warriors,*
> *Many a mead-hall filled with festive life,*
> *Until mighty fate overturned all.*
> *Far and wide the slaughtered fell, the plague-days came,*
> *Death snatched away all the host of men.*
> *Their battlements became waste places,*
> *The citadel crumbled.*

9

The Wanderer, a poem which treats of the misery of exile, contains a formal lament for the lost delights of the noble life:

> *Where is the horse? Where the hero? Where the treasure-giving prince?*
> *Where the seats at the feast, where the delights of the hall?*
> *Alas, bright goblet! Alas, mailed fighter!*
> *Alas, princely power. How that time has passed away,*
> *Grown dark beneath night's helmet, as though it had not been.*

The Rhyming Poem of the Exeter Book begins by telling of the good life, nobleman guiding ship or horse, living amid courtly pleasures, surrounded by a devoted retinue. It ends with the decline of life and its joys, with death and judgment.

The great poet who composed *Beowulf* used this poignant contrast between thriving and decaying as a technical device to point his tragedy. Often, amidst his descriptions of brightness and gaiety, he gives a hint of future darkness. He shows the Danish king Hrothgar building a great and glittering palace, and holding his first court in it. At this moment, the moment of creation, the poet reminds his hearers of how short the life of the hall is to be: 'It awaited the tumult of battle, the hostile flame' which was soon to destroy it. Later, after Beowulf has defended the hall against the intruding murderous monster Grendel, Hrothgar holds a feast. He and his nephew Hrothulf, co-rulers, preside. The scene is one of gaiety and harmony, but when the poet mentions these two princely figures together, he adds such comments as 'at that time the Danes were not committing treachery' and 'their kinship was still a real thing, each one loyal to the other', sardonic hints at Hrothulf's coming violation of faith in grasping the throne as sole monarch.

e slaughtered fell'

To speak as I have done in this chapter is, of course, to stress unduly the darker side of Anglo-Saxon life. Of course there were times of pleasure, happiness and peace, as other parts of the literature show. But it is important to remember the background of everyday violence which, even yet, we do not experience, and which demanded in man a wariness, a readiness to defend, a need to be prepared for disaster, and perhaps a resignation to the dispensations of fate or the inscrutable will of God—*The Wanderer* closes with the words: 'Well it is for the man who seeks grace, solace from the Father in the heavens, where all our security lies.'

When Alfred complained of the manifold cares of the king's office, or compared his lot with that of the countryman living contentedly winter and summer 'as I have not yet been able to do', he spoke as a man of sufferings; as a man who had borne chronic illness since adolescence; as a prince who had seen three older brothers in turn succeed to the throne of Wessex and die after short reigns; as a war-leader who, in the year 871 alone, had experienced nine pitched battles against the Danish host, and who in his turn had put to sea with his fleet to engage the enemy afloat; as a king who had been driven by Viking marauders into the wastes of his land, where he inspired and organised counter-attack and resistance. His biographer, bishop Asser, speaks of him as 'harassed night and day by so many diseases unknown to all the doctors of this island, and also by internal and external anxieties of sovereignty and by invasions of the heathen by sea and land'. St Cuthbert, who chose for himself the hard and austere life of fasting, watching and prayer, was a victim of the plague, whose effects he bore for the rest of his life. When his body was examined in the nineteenth century

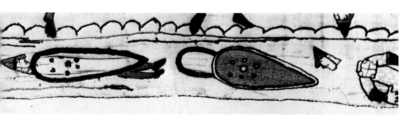

it was found to be highly tubercular, and the early biographies show him suffering from diseases of undernourishment, from tumours on knee, foot and groin. These two men, leaders of church and state, were exceptional Anglo-Saxons, but their situations were not exceptional, and they form an appropriate introduction to a description of the life of the times. The historian Gibbon, whose ideal of civilisation derived from the Golden Age of the Antonines, defined early Anglo-Saxon England succinctly as 'seven independent kingdoms . . . agitated by perpetual discord'. There is enough truth in the aphorism to make it effective.

This eleventh-century rune-stone at Yttergärde, Uppland, Sweden, commemorates the Viking Ulfr who took part in the attacks on England. It records proudly that he shared in three payments of danegeld *during his fighting career*

Further Reading

The standard history is F. M. Stenton, *Anglo-Saxon England* (2nd ed.), 1947 (Oxford History of England, vol. 2). A good beginning is P. H. Blair, *An Introduction to Anglo-Saxon England*, while D. M. Wilson, *The Anglo-Saxons*, stresses the archaeological background. For translations of many of the texts that I quote (though for Old English material I tend to use my own translations), see *English Historical Documents*, vol. 1 ed. by Dorothy Whitelock, vol. 2 by D. C. Douglas and G. W. Greenaway. The *Anglo-Saxon Chronicle* text of these two volumes is published separately, ed. by Dorothy Whitelock, and there is also a convenient cheap translation by G. N. Garmonsway in Everyman's Library. W. Bonser, *The Medical Background of Anglo-Saxon England*, gives a mass of material on famine, plague and the expectation of life.

II

The World of the Anglo-Saxons

The land the Anglo-Saxons occupied was startlingly different from our own. There were different political boundaries. Internally, for part of our period, the country was split into a number of states, more or less independent, with a few enclaves of Britons like those of the Yorkshire kingdom of Elmet which survived until the seventh century. In the ninth century half the country came under the power of invading Viking armies and the hosts of peasants who settled under their protection. The Scandinavian king of York often had closer contacts with Ireland than he had with southern England. The land boundaries, too, shifted. Even after the early period of conquest, settlement and consolidation, three remained long unfixed: those with the Britons of Wales and Cornwall, and that in the north which must be guarded against a variety of hostile peoples. In the seventh century the line of the Welsh boundary was tentatively drawn,

Offa's Dyke near Mainstone, Salop

A cluster of gravestones from the Anglo-Saxon monastery of Whithorn

but Offa's Dyke, constructed in the second half of the eighth, represents a revision. There were later English inroads deep into Wales, and some Welsh princes admitted the overlordship of Anglo-Saxon kings. Not until the ninth century was the westward push into Cornwall complete. The northern marches were turbulent. The Anglians occupied Lothian in the seventh century, and the Scots slowly pushed them out again in the tenth. By the seventh century the English controlled much of south-west Scotland and certainly the Solway coastline as far as Wigtownshire, but by the tenth they had even lost large parts of north-west England.

Geographically, too, there were major differences. The great roads that the Romans had built remained, though their state of repair must have declined. Watling Street led from London to Wroxeter, whence a branch continued to Chester. Ermine Street joined London to Lincoln, and so to the Humber and York. The Fosse Way ran across country from Lincoln to Bath and then to Devon, while there were many smaller Roman roads, as well as the great traditional routes like the Icknield Way, from East Anglia via the Chilterns to the west country, which are non-Roman in origin. Despite the existence of these roads, movement through the land was difficult. There was much more heavy woodland than there is now. The great forest called the Weald (Old English *Andredesweald*) stretched, according to the *Chronicle* for 892, 'from east to west 120 miles long or longer, and 30 miles broad', an extent that was traversed by

14

only three roads, to Chichester, to Lewes and to the Sussex coast. North of the Thames, from Essex to the Chilterns, spread the great forest which survives fragmentarily as Epping and Hainault. In Huntingdonshire and Northamptonshire was *Bruneswald*, whose name remains in place-names with the element Bromswold. In the west, between Wiltshire and Somerset, lay Selwood, where Alfred took refuge in time of great distress. Forests such as these—and there were many others, as well as less extensive woodlands and coppices—both formed a physical barrier to communication, and also sheltered bands of footpads, like that described in a north-country lair in Aethelwulf's poem *De Abbatibus:* 'an evil band, an object for wrath, rushing this way and that in their fleetness . . . hiding in the thick bushes, ever confident when under offensive arms . . . laying ambushes for many'. Across eastern England stretched another barrier to movement, the great undrained fens. St Guthlac's biographer reports that this district 'begins at the banks of the river Granta, not far from . . . Cambridge, and stretches from the south as far north as the sea. It is a very long tract, now consisting of marshes, now of bogs, sometimes of black waters overhung by fog, sometimes studded with wooded islands and traversed by windings of tortuous streams.'

In a country like this communications were difficult, dangerous and slow. Rivers were extensively used, so that many inland towns were ports reached by rivers no longer commercially navigable. In 894 a Viking fleet rowed up the Lea, 20 miles above London. In 1013 Swein's ships sailed up the Trent as far as Gainsborough. When earl Godwine's men seized prince Alfred, son of Aethelred the Unready, at Guildford, they took him to his hideous captivity in Ely by ship. The monks of ?South Shields rafted their building timber from the forests down the river Tyne to the monastery site. York was a vital centre of northern English trade, and finds there show links with the great Scandinavian marts of Birka, Sweden, and Hedeby, Schleswig. During the late Anglo-Saxon period the citizens built extensive drainage and embanking works intended to make the marshy site more habitable, and to allow goods to be unloaded from ships more easily. Yet rivers could be formidable barriers, too,

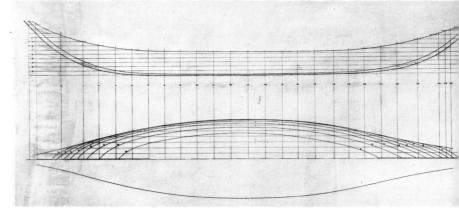

The Anglo-Saxon ship found at Sutton Hoo

as the charter emphasis on the duty of bridge-building implies. When Swein's army left Winchester for London in 1013, they had trouble crossing the Thames, 'and many of his host were drowned . . . because they did not trouble to find a bridge'. It is hard to say how quickly it was possible to travel in such a land, for the evidence is slight and is usually confined to special cases. According to Bede's *Life of St Cuthbert*, the news of the Northumbrian disaster at *Nechtanesmere*, near Forfar, took two days by express messenger to reach the monastery near Carlisle where Cuthbert received it, a distance of about 150 miles. In 1066 Harold, making his forced march down the major routes from York to London on his way to death at Hastings, took four or five days over the 190 miles. These were journeys where speed was important, and trained personnel were involved. Local travel, travel by people ignorant of the roads, travel through difficult country or with heavy loads, must have taken longer unless there were a navigable river handy to help.

In these circumstances many Anglo-Saxon settlements must have been remote to a degree we find hard to imagine. When travelling in the morning through the north border country—the earliest version of the tale takes place at Chester-le-Street—St Cuthbert called in at a lonely farmhouse for a rest. The farmer's wife invited him to stay for a meal: 'You will not find another village on your way, nor even a house, and it will take you till sunset to reach your destination.' As a pastor Cuthbert would walk or ride through the wild regions round Melrose, preaching

16

especially 'in those villages that were far away on steep and rugged mountains, which others dreaded to visit, and whose poverty as well as ignorance prevented teachers from approaching them'. The marshlands were so empty that the chronicler for 1010 remarked as though with surprise that Thorkel's Vikings 'even went into the wild fens' of East Anglia, plundering and burning. St Guthlac's biographer describes the hermitage site at Crowland, 'which, on account of the wildness of this very remote district, had hitherto remained untilled and known to very few'.

In districts like these, in the new clearings in forests or in the occasional island colonies, life must have been very circumscribed, in-bred and monotonous, with visitors few and settlements largely self-supporting. Indeed, this seclusion was sometimes the occasion for settlement. Cuthbert lived for a time on the Farne Islands, his hut fenced round by a turf and stone wall high enough to restrict his view and keep his wandering thoughts in check. The Irishman Fursa was given the enclosed site of a deserted fortress, probably Burgh Castle in Suffolk, for his hermitage and the monastery which succeeded it.

Burgh Castle, Suffolk

Even in the more populous districts, life was by modern standards narrow and interests were restricted, but here there must have been a good deal of coming and going, with interchange of news and ideas, and with opportunities for buying exotic produce and artefacts. Bede's praise of Edwin's control of his kingdom, that a woman with a new-born babe could travel securely from coast to coast, implies that such a journey was possible, however unlikely to be carried out in those circumstances. Bede added that 'in many places where he saw clear springs near the highways, Edwin had stakes fixed, with bronze cups hanging on them, for the refreshment of wayfarers', and this, too, suggests that travelling was common.

How wide was a man's world in one of these districts? What chance would he have to meet people, how far would he be likely to go from home, what idea might he have of distant lands or nations? Passing through the countryside from royal estate to royal estate came the king and his retinue, at any rate after the kingly office had achieved some magnitude and dignity. The nobleman conducted a more modest progress of the same sort. The king could summon his council to meet at one of his estates, and this would bring the leading figures of church and state across country, perhaps camping in tents if the weather was clement. Athelstan is known to have held his court in 17 places in Devon, Somerset, Dorset, Wiltshire, Hampshire, Berkshire, Sussex, Surrey and Kent, as well as at such places north of the Thames as York, Tamworth, Buckingham, Whittlebury, Colchester and London. A bishop might make a pastoral visitation with his staff and servants—even the austere Cuthbert had enough attendants to make accommodation a difficulty in the wild mountains, 'so the people put up tents for him, and for themselves they made huts of felled branches as best they could'. Alcuin complained that archbishop Eanbald II of York took too many attendants and servants wherever he travelled, and so embarrassed the monasteries which had to put them all up. Many others, too, travelled on religious business. The parish priest visited his bishop to fetch holy oil. Sick or injured attended famed shrines in the hope of remedy. St Cuthbert's at Lindisfarne saw the cures of two boys, one a demoniac and the other a paralytic, who were carried on wagons to the island, and a blind man from the province of Wissa on the lower Nene was shipped to Crowland to be healed at Guthlac's grave. The king's servants might pass through a village, claiming lodging as was their right. We hear of these in the charters. A grant by Ceolwulf I of Mercia of land at *Mylentun*, Kent, freed archbishop Wulfred from 'entertainment of king, bishop, ealdormen, or of reeves, tax-gatherers, keepers of dogs, horses or hawks, from feeding or support of all those who are called *fæstingmen*', the last word a technical term for some rank of royal official. On giving to bishop Ealhhun of Worcester the monastery of Blockley, Burgred of Mercia freed it from the responsibility of feeding, maintaining and lodging the Welsh expedition (? men who patrolled the Welsh marches; ? the king's messengers into Wales), and from 'lodging all mounted men of the English race and foreigners, whether of noble or humble birth'. Unofficially journeying through the country would be the merchant or pedlar whose activities some of the law-codes regulate. The laws of Hlothhere and Eadric of Kent define the responsibility of a host for the good behaviour of 'a stranger, trader or any other man who has come across the frontier'. Those of Ine have provisions to protect a merchant from the accusation of stealing. If he buys goods *uppe on folce*, 'from people in the countryside', he must have proper witnesses. Alfred's laws try to check people of dubious character from traversing the land masquerading as traders. A merchant must take before the king's reeve the men who are to accompany him, and must be prepared to bring any of them to justice if they commit an offence.

In these ways Anglo-Saxons, even of humble station, could meet strangers and so learn something of the life of men outside.

Ox-carts

By these ways foreign goods and materials could penetrate remote parts of England—the fragment of eastern glassware (perhaps from Egypt) found in a barrow at Cheesecake Hill in east Yorkshire, for instance. Probably this is the only contact many Anglo-Saxons had with another world. But sometimes men had to leave their settlements and travel. Even a slave could be bought and sold, and for much of the Anglo-Saxon period the freeman could move without restriction. He might be called up for military service, and have to fight at least as far afield as his shire extended, and sometimes even farther. The *Chronicle* for 893 shows Alfred leading his section of the West Saxon levies to besiege a Viking army which had taken refuge on an island in the river Colne, just west of London. The Scandinavians of East Anglia and Northumbria made a diversionary attack on Exeter, drawing most of Alfred's men westward again to relieve the town. The rest of his army marched east to London, and thence, reinforced, advanced and stormed the enemy fortress at Benfleet, Essex. Byrhtnoth's force, defeated by the Vikings at Maldon, Essex, in 991, certainly included local men such as Leofsunu of Sturmer, but also Aelfwine who was of Mercian stock, and Aescferth, a hostage from Northumbria. A freeman might travel for other reasons, to attend folk-meetings or legal assemblies at the hundred-place, the shire-meeting or a local court. In the later period, when the king's coinage was carefully regulated and called in at fixed intervals, a wealthy man might have to attend the nearest mint-town to exchange old coins for new. A man might wish to buy or sell goods, obeying Edward the Elder's edict that nobody should conduct this business *butan porte*, 'save in a market-town' and with the witness of the reeve or of other trustworthy people. There he might meet traders from abroad, like the Frisians who had a colony in York in the eighth century, or the men from Rouen who imported

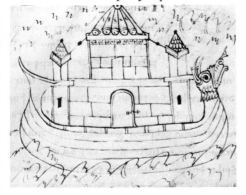

Noah's ark, drawn on the model of a contemporary ship

wine and blubber fish into Billingsgate in the eleventh.

From the earliest times the Anglo-Saxons had trading relations with the continent. Early Kentish culture is closely linked to those of Scandinavia and Frankland. The gold, electrum and silver coins called *sceattas*, minted in south-east England in the seventh century, appear in continental hoards, while Netherlandish moneyers copied their designs for a coinage which was current on both sides of the Channel. Pottery and glass were imported from the Rhineland, the Low Countries and northern France, some of it in connection with a trade in wine. Techniques, too, were brought to England —the so-called Ipswich pottery ware

Seventh-century sceattas, *obverse and reverse. The top two are English, the third is a Continental copy*

is influenced by that of the Rhineland—and there may even have been immigrant workmen, glass-makers from north France and Belgium employed in the south of England. In turn Saxon merchants visited the annual fair at St Denis, near Paris. In 796 Charles the Great complained to Offa of Mercia that English merchants were trying to avoid paying toll by mixing with pilgrims passing through his territory. At the same time he made some pointed comments on the mini-size' of cloaks which were being exported from England, and a demand for a return to the old fashion. There was an English merchant at Marseilles in the eighth century. In the ninth a certain Wulfstan, presumably an Englishman, told Alfred of his trading ventures into the Baltic, where he called at Hedeby, the great mart near modern Schleswig, and at another port seven days' sail along the Baltic, at the mouth of the Vistula. Throughout the Anglo-Saxon period, then, Englishmen were meeting merchants from Scandinavia, north Germany, the Netherlands and the Frankish seaboard, so that foreign goods came to the southern and eastern ports like London, Southampton, Ipswich and Norwich from such centres as

Byzantine silver from Sutton Hoo

Dorestad (Wijk-bij-Duurstede, Netherlands), Quentovic (Étaples or somewhere in its neighbourhood), Wissant and Cologne. These intermediaries gave the inland Anglo-Saxon some idea of worlds far distant from their own; witness the elephant ivory playing-pieces from the cemetery at Caistor-by-Norwich, the Byzantine silver of the Sutton Hoo treasure, the

eastern textiles in St Cuthbert's tomb, and the Arabic dinar which Offa of Mercia copied in a prestige issue of gold.

Commerce was not the only way of bringing England and the continent together. There was a lot of diplomatic contact

Offa of Mercia's copy of a dinar of Caliph Al Mansur. The engraver has copied, with some error, the Arabic inscriptions, and has added the legend OFFA REX upside-down with respect to the Arabic

formalised by the arranged marriages which linked Anglo-Saxon and foreign royal houses. Aethelberht of Kent married Bertha, daughter of the Merovingian Charibert. To England she brought her chaplain, bishop Liudhard, and her retinue may have included the moneyer Eusebius who struck coins at Canterbury. Aethelwulf of Wessex married the 13 year-old Judith, daughter of Charles the Bald, king of the West Franks. Charles the Great and Offa of Mercia haggled unsuccessfully about a contract between their offspring. Aelfthryth, daughter of Alfred, was the wife of Baldwin II, count of Flanders, and the alliance thus established lasted several decades. Several of Edward the Elder's daughters were married abroad: Eadgyfu to Charles the Simple, Eadgyth to the Emperor Otto the Great, Eadhild to Hugh the Great, duke of the Franks, Aelfgyfu perhaps to Conrad the Peaceable of Burgundy, and a second Eadgyfu to Lewis of Lower Burgundy. Aethelred the Unready's second wife was Emma, daughter of Richard I of Normandy. She subsequently married Cnut the Great. Cnut's daughter Gunnhild married Henry, who was to become the Emperor Henry III. Athelstan made alliances by fostering at his court the sons of his fellow princes: Hakon, son of Harald the Fine-haired of Norway; Lewis, son of Charles the Simple; Alan who later was count of Brittany. In 936 and 939 he mounted expeditions to help Alan and Lewis regain lost territory.

More significant still in connecting England with the continent was the Christian religion. Aethelberht's marriage to Bertha brought Rome to southern England. The link, once forged, remained fast. To Rome went the English tribute of Peter's pence. To Rome went the English archbishops or their deputies to claim the *pallia* which the Pope bestowed. To Rome

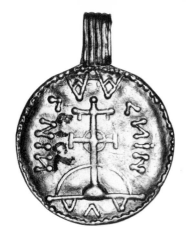

Medalet of bishop Liudhard: the obverse has a retrograde legend giving his name and title, LEVDARDVS·EPS

travelled pilgrims in such numbers that Charles the Great provided the cell of Saint-Josse-sur-Mer, near Quentovic, 'for hospitality towards pilgrims and strangers', and Boniface warned of the moral dangers awaiting Englishwomen who made the perilous journey through France, Switzerland and Italy. To Rome journeyed young and enthusiastic clerics, like Benedict Biscop and St Wilfrid, bringing back books, vestments, holy pictures, as well as workmen, masons and glaziers. From Rome came the letters, replies, exhortations and rebukes of the Pope. From Rome in 668 came Theodore of Tarsus to become archbishop of Canterbury and preside over the reorganisation of the church. From Rome came the papal legates of 786, bringing plans for reform of the English church, and meeting here the great scholar Alcuin, home on leave from his directorship of the palace school of Charles the Great. The road to Rome was a well-trodden one, and some of those who took it were kings, Cenred and Burgred of Mercia, Ceadwalla and Ine of Wessex, Offa of Essex. Luckily there survives the itinerary of bishop Sigeric who returned from the eternal city in the 990s. He travelled via Viterbo, Lucca, Piacenza, Vercelli, Aosta, across the Great St Bernard Pass, through Lausanne, Besançon, Brienne, Châlons, Reims, Laon, Arras, and so apparently to Wissant where he boarded ship for England. The route was a dangerous one. Bishop Aelfsige of Winchester died of cold in the

24

Alps. Ruffians ambushed and robbed the harmless bishop Winfrith of Lichfield, mistaking him for the more famous St Wilfrid who was journeying to Rome at the same time.

Beyond Rome the pilgrim route led to the Holy Land, but few Anglo-Saxons followed it so far. Elsewhere on the continent, however, the English church was active, bringing the true faith to benighted heathens in Frisia and western and central Germany. Such missionaries as Wilfrid, Willibrord, Boniface, Willehad and Lull toiled in the Netherlands, in Saxony, Hesse, Thuringia and Bavaria, their work often bringing heavenly glory but earthly disaster. Two of them, both called Hewald and therefore distinguished by the epithets 'black' and 'white', tried to convert the Old Saxons who promptly martyred them. In old age Boniface returned to the mission field; pagans killed him at Dokkum, near the Frisian coast. These missionaries kept close ties with Rome, and some of them, Boniface for example, collaborated with the Frankish church. The religious houses they founded, adopted or influenced—Utrecht, Echternach, Bremen, Kaiserswerth, Fulda, Tauberbischofsheim, Mainz, St Gall, Reichenau—formed centres of English culture abroad, and many of them kept up the English connection. The surviving letters of Boniface, Lull, his disciple who became archbishop of Mainz, and later of Alcuin, whom Charles the Great lured from York to become his teacher and confidant, suggest a lively intercourse between these exiled clerics and their stay-at-home brethren. Boniface and Lull write home for advice and consolation, and for the books which they cannot get in Germany. To Eadburh, abbess of Minster, Thanet, Boniface sends the priest Eofa carrying gold to be used in decorating a copy of St Peter's epistles which she is making for him. To Daniel, bishop of Winchester, goes the priest Forthhere with letters and 'small gifts as a token of pure love; namely a cloak, not of pure silk but mixed with goat's wool, and a towel for drying your feet'. Lull sends to his former master Dealwine 'some poor little gifts . . . not worthy of you but sent with a devoted heart.' In return he asks for copies of Aldhelm's writings. Cuthbert, abbot of Wearmouth, asks Lull if he knows anyone who can make glass vessels. If so, will he urge him to cross the sea to Wearmouth, 'because we are ignorant and destitute of that art'. Can he also send a harpist, as Cuthbert has a harp but no player. Even letters like these record the sense of isolation which distance brought in the Middle Ages. Cuthbert remarks that six years ago he sent Lull some gifts by a priest Hunwine who was travelling in that direction. Hunwine died on the way, and Cuthbert has not yet heard whether the presents reached their destination. Such an anecdote illustrates the two faces of Anglo-Saxon England. It was intimately connected with western Europe, and through it was linked to the mysterious and remote countries of the east. At the same time it was a solitary land, where people lived cut off from their fellows by time, distance and the difficulties and dangers of travelling. Yes.

Further Reading

An excellent account of trading connections between England and other countries is in H. R. Loyn, *Anglo-Saxon England and the Norman Conquest*, a book which is good on most aspects of Anglo-Saxon social history. There are several works which give more specialised treatment to the subject: S. J. Crawford, *Anglo-Saxon Influence on Western Christendom, 600–800*; W. Levison, *England and the Continent in the Eighth Century;* G. C. Dunning, 'Trade Relationships between England and the Continent in the Late Anglo-Saxon Period', in D. B. Harden, *Dark Age Britain.* Early accounts of St Cuthbert are translated in Bertram Colgrave, *Two Lives of Saint Cuthbert.*

III

Gods and Demons, Witches, Magicians and Monsters

For the first century and a half after their arrival, the Anglo-Saxons were pagans. For their last 400 years of rule they were Christians. On the whole formal conversion was rapid and complete, though some kingdoms, like Sussex, long held the old religion, while others, like Essex, witnessed occasional relapses from the new faith. Nearly all extant Anglo-Saxon texts are post-conversion, when paganism was regarded with horror and disgust. Most were written by professional Christians whose aim was to suppress memory of former beliefs rather than to record them with care or antiquarian curiosity. Hence we know little of Anglo-Saxon heathendom, and that little is more in the nature of slight hints and minute snippets of information than an ordered or coherent account of the religion. As a consequence scholars have often appealed to the richer sources available for other Germanic peoples—especially the Scandinavians, who possess an extensive medieval record of pagan myth and worship—and have assumed them relevant to Anglo-Saxon belief. Such an approach can be fruitful and suggestive, but it demands caution. Intervals of time and place are important even in a medieval context, and there is enough evidence of variations of belief and cult within Scandinavia itself to suggest that England, partly isolated as it was in development, had its own versions of Germanic paganism.

We know the names of several Anglo-Saxon gods and goddesses. Tiw, Woden, Thunor and Frig gave their names to days of the week. Since all have Scandinavian parallels (Týr,

Óthin, Thór and Frigg) we can suggest their attributes with some chance of accuracy. Óthin is linked with battle and the dead, with magic and the arts of incantation and poetry, and with the curious Germanic script called runic. The slender Anglo-Saxon evidence suggests the same for Woden. According to the tenth-century chronicler Aethelweard he was a dead hero taken as a god, to whom pagans 'offered sacrifice in order to have victory or be courageous'. Woden's name is mysteriously invoked in an imperfectly Christianised and poorly preserved charm against the venom of serpents and flying infection, the *Nine Herbs Charm:* 'A serpent came slithering: it devoured ? a man. Then Woden took nine glory-twigs, and struck the adder so that it flew into nine fragments.' This passage, obscure in itself, has no clear link to what precedes or follows. It comes after a short section which mentions a wise and holy prince who hung in the heavens; the obvious reading of this is as a reference to Christ who hung upon the cross, but Scandinavian myth knows of a time when Óthin hung, for nine nights, on a wind-swept tree, and so achieved magical secrets and powers.

A gnomic verse says cryptically: 'Woden made idols; the Almighty made glory, the spacious heavens. He is the powerful God, the true king himself, saviour of souls.' Here Woden may have been turned into a devil who led men's souls astray, but there is such marked contrast between him as creator and the creating God as to suggest that, in Anglo-Saxon as in Norse myth, Woden became pre-eminent among pagan deities, perhaps the universal father.

We know little about Tiw. Even for Týr, his Norse equivalent, information is scanty, though he seems to have been a god of war or of death, and to have governed legal process and agreement. One of the characters of the runic alphabet, ↑, has the name *tir* which scholars connect with *Týr, Tiw*. The use of this character is suggestive. It was cut on some of the cremation urns buried at Loveden Hill in Lincolnshire, and this may represent invocation of the god of death, whose power could support the deceased or perhaps protect the living from his attentions. On each end of a sixth-century sword pommel from Faversham, Kent, is a pattern which looks like the rune *tir*,

Sword-pommel from Faversham, showing the tir *rune*

engraved and blackened with niello. The Norse poem, *Sigrdrífumál*, admittedly of rather later date, has the verse: 'If you want victory, learn victory runes and cut them on your sword hilt, some on the ?hilt sockets, some on the ?pommel bars, and name Týr twice.' Despite divergency of place and date, the Faversham pommel suggests a two-fold invocation of Tiw strikingly in accord with that of *Sigrdrífumál*, the god of war called upon to strengthen or protect the sword's owner. The 'lightning flashes' and perhaps the swastikas too, on other early swords may be appeals to Thunor, equivalent to Thór, the Scandinavian god of thunder and of natural power, who was also a doughty fighter.

Less well known to moderns than these gods is Seaxnet, who appears in the genealogies of the kings of Essex, and who, as Saxnot, is named in the Old Saxon formula listing the demons the Christian convert is required to renounce. In his *De Ratione Temporum* Bede mentions two goddesses, Hreda/Hretha and Eostre, in whose honour are named the months in which their festivals occur, March (*Hredmonath*) and April (*Eosturmonath*), the second surviving in the Christian festival, Easter. A charm to make land more fruitful invokes Erce, who is described as 'mother of earth' and is presumably a fertility deity. One of the letters of the runic alphabet is called *Ing*, a word defined in *The Runic Poem* thus: 'Among the East-Danes Ing was first seen by men, until he departed east [some scholars amend to 'west'] across the sea. His chariot ran behind him. Thus the Heardings named the warrior.' From Scandinavian sources we learn that Ing, or Yngvi, was another name for the great fertility god Freyr, who seems to have been worshipped

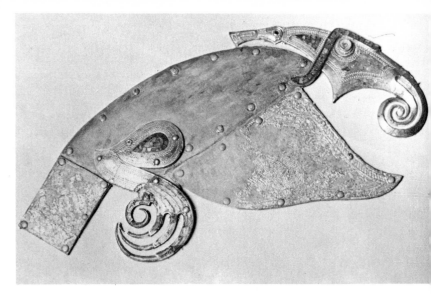

Sutton Hoo bird

in the low-lying areas by the North Sea whence some of the Anglo-Saxon peoples came. The chariot which *The Runic Poem* mentions so obscurely may be some sort of wagon trundled through the fields which the god was asked to bless and make fruitful—the practice is known from continental and northern Germania.

Further discussion of Anglo-Saxon paganism is largely speculative. In the figures on the plates of the helmet from Sutton Hoo, Suffolk, some scholars have seen evidence of Woden worship, and the decorative bird on the accompanying shield has been linked to the same god, the Raven-god as the Norsemen called him. The great unused whetstone, also found at Sutton Hoo, is assumed to have served ceremonial purposes, and the fact that Norse myth connects Thór with a whetstone, part of which he bears embedded in his forehead, has led some to suggest a Thunor cult.

A boar's image stands as a crest on the crown of the helmet from Benty Grange, Derbyshire, while boars also adorn the cheek guards of the Sutton Hoo specimen. *Beowulf* describes this type of helmet decoration: 'Figures of boars, gold-adorned, shining, hardened in the fire, glittered over their cheek-pieces.

The warlike beast guarded the lives of the fierce warriors.' In Scandinavian mythology the boar is Freyr's beast. Freyr was a mighty warrior, and to use his symbol might be a way of gaining his protection in battle. If so, the owner of the Benty Grange helmet had double insurance, for it also bears Christ's cross.

The boar on the Benty Grange helmet

Finally, scholars have appealed to place-names for information on the relative popularity of individual gods and on geographical distribution of cults. Most frequent in English place-names are Woden, Thunor and Tiw; their cults seem strongest in the central Midlands, central south and southeast. There are, for example, such place-names as Wednesbury, 'Woden's *burh* or fortification', Wensley (Derbyshire), 'Woden's grove'; Wansdyke, 'Woden's ditch'; Thunderfield, 'Thunor's open land'; Thundridge, 'Thunor's ridge'; Tuesley, 'Tiw's grove'; Tysoe, 'Tiw's hill-spur'. Many of these are thought to be centres of worship, particularly if the god-name has a suitable second element, such as 'grove', or if there is contributory evidence as at Tysoe, where an early record reports the existence of a hill-figure of a horse, appropriate in Germanic terms to the cult-centre of a god of war

The Sutton Hoo helmet

or death. Occasionally a place-name contains a clue as to a god's nature. Thurstable means 'Thunor's pillar', and hence it is likely that the locals worshipped Thunor in connection with a great column which was represented as supporting the sky or the world.

This much we know of the Anglo-Saxon gods, but of the forms of worship, of the ways they affected daily life, we know almost nothing. Bede says that February was called *Solmonath*, the month of cakes (*placentae*) which they offered to their gods. No Old English word *sol*, 'cake', is known, and Bede, writing after several decades of Christian practice in northern England, may have misinterpreted his information. In March and April were held the feasts of Hreda and Eostre. September was called *Halegmonath*, 'holy month', and October/November *Blodmonath* (*Bloth-*, *Blot-*), 'month of sacrifice', 'because in it they dedicated to their gods the beasts they would kill'. The night which began the New Year—about our Christmas—was called *Modranect*, 'mothers' night', because, or so Bede suspected, of certain ceremonies held at the time. Various historical sources mention idols to whom offerings were made, and there is some suggestion in the penitentials of sacrificial feasts such as were celebrated in pagan Scandinavia. Sacred places were often groves, woodlands and clearings, and, though temples are occasionally mentioned, we know little of them. We know little, too, of the priesthood, whether it was professional or a part-time occupation. Bede tell us how Coifi, chief priest (*primus pontificum*, a title which suggests there were ranks of priesthood) of the Northumbrians, expected worldly honours and rewards to accompany his sacred office. In disgust at his ill success he renounced paganism in favour of the Christianity which Paulinus preached, and eagerly led the people to destroy the temple at Goodmanham, Yorkshire. Bearing arms, he mounted a stallion to ride to the attack, 'for it had been unlawful for a priest either to bear arms or to ride anything but a mare'. Place-names add a few facts about organisation, from which it seems that temples played differing roles in the people's worship. In 767 Harrow on the Hill was called *Gumeninga hergae*, 'temple of the Gumenings, the people of Guma', implying that this was an important cult-place for a group or tribe.

On the other hand Peper Harrow, Surrey, seems to mean 'temple of the man called Pippera', which suggests that the shrine was privately owned, perhaps by a leading farmer who levied tax upon those who attended, as happened later in Iceland.

It is unlikely that Anglo-Saxon heathenism had any strong intellectual content, for it was readily cast aside in favour of Christianity, which had a coherent doctrine and which supplied answers to some of the difficulties which Anglo-Saxon man faced. Again Bede is our authority for a few comments made by pagans on their religion, and Bede, of course, was prejudiced. Expounding his discontent with paganism, Coifi picked upon two points, one practical, one philosophical. He complained that, though he had served the gods most zealously, he had got little reward: 'If the gods were any good, they would rather want to benefit *me*, since I have taken greater care to serve them.' This is a crude and materialistic religious attitude, expecting the deities to grant worldly favour to those who cultivate them. Coifi's intellectual discontent is expressed in his reaction to hearing Paulinus's preaching of the gospel: 'For some time I have realised that there was nothing in the cult we practised, because, you see, the more earnestly I sought truth in it, the less I found it. But now I confess openly that there is such obvious truth in that teaching [of Paulinus] as to confer upon us the gifts of life, salvation and eternal happiness.' There is a similar emptiness implied in the picture which one of Edwin's counsellors drew of the life of man under paganism. He compared it to the flight of a sparrow across a banqueting hall during a winter feast. The bird enters from darkness, and flies out into darkness, and it is the same with man's life, 'for of what follows or what went before, we know nothing'. Of course, we do not know if Bede's account of the scene is accurate, nor if these pagans reacted typically to their religion. Certainly it was probably materialistic, the aim of worship being to ensure protection, fertility, prosperity and so on. The Northumbrian counsellor's comment is, however, not convincing. It indicates that pagan religion had no firm teaching about the after-life, which seems unlikely from the evidence of early

33

Incised and inscribed urns from Loveden Hill

cemeteries in various parts of the country. With the bodies or the ashes of the deceased, the heathen Anglo-Saxons often buried grave goods, jewels, weapons, utensils, playing-pieces, sometimes food and animals. Sometimes the goods were specially made for burial. Surely the pagans must have believed that the dead needed these things, and made use of them in some future life resembling that on this earth.

So far I have discussed the formal side of paganism, an official religion with widespread organisation and an accepted pantheon. But, as in Scandinavia, there must also have existed, side by side with it, less formal cults: fertility rites such as continued in attenuated form right up to the present century, local deities, cults of the family which linked to a belief in the power of the dead. Not only gods were worshipped, but also natural features. The penitential of archbishop Theodore forbids votive offerings to trees, springs, stones and rocks, and other penitentials and some legal codes repeat the prohibition. A charter mentions an ash-tree 'which the ignorant call holy'. Fertility practices occur in some charms. The rune-inscribed urns of the Loveden Hill, Lincolnshire, cremation cemetery may show a cult of the dead. And there were probably local or minor deities or supernatural beings of lesser standing similar to those malignant spirits who are exorcised in a charm against ? rheumatism. The sudden pains of this disease were

34

caused by the spears or arrows shot by female demons who are described thus:

> *Loud were they, lo! loud, as they rode over the mound.*
> *Fierce they were as they rode over the land.*
> *Shield you now if you are to survive this vicious attack.*
> *Out, little spear, if you are in here!*
> *I stood beneath the lime-wood, beneath the light shield*
> *Where the mighty women betrayed their powers,*
> *And, yelling, sent forth their spears. . . .*

On the evidence of place-names of the 'animal-head' type (for example, Gateshead, 'goat's head', Broxhead, 'badger's head', Eversheds, 'boar's head'), some scholars have urged that the pagan Anglo-Saxons followed a practice recorded elsewhere in Germania, that of sacrificing animals to their gods and placing the heads on poles, which thus marked cult-places. There could be a link here, too, with the occasional grave-finds of animals' heads, like the pig's head carefully placed between flat stones at Frilford, Berkshire, and the ox-skull buried in a pit at Soham, Cambridgeshire.

The conversion to Christianity must have put a quick end to the more formal side of paganism, but right through Anglo-Saxon times authorities were sufficiently worried about a revival to fulminate against the religion in homilies, and to strike at it in their law-codes. This may be partly due to fear that invading Vikings would infect Christian minds with their own version of Germanic paganism, but part was the result of lingering heathen practices among the people. In the decades following conversion many must have been confused about the distinction between Christ and the old gods, as was king Redwald of East Anglia who, in the same building had an altar dedicated to Christ and another, little,

Trouble with elves

35

one (*arula*, perhaps a diminutive of contempt in Bede's usage) on which victims were offered to devils. Certainly, the early mass conversions, such as those which Paulinus achieved in Northumbria, could hardly have led to sophisticated understanding of Christian doctrine, and it is not surprising that pagan practices continued. People did not stop burying grave-goods when they turned Christian. Though late Anglo-Saxon graves are unfurnished and so hard to date, some of the richest graves are in fact post-conversion. And in many other ways superstitions from a pre-Christian era persisted to the end of Anglo-Saxon England.

In its decline, and in accounts of Christian writers, paganism was often identified with magic. In his *Life of St Wilfrid* Eddius describes the saint's shipwreck on the Sussex coast. The inhabitants, heathen even as late as the end of the seventh century, attacked the survivors, trying to steal their belongings. Their chief priest (*princeps sacerdotum idolatriae*, later also called *magus*, 'magician') stood on a high mound chanting curses upon the people of God, trying thereby to bind their hands. According to Bede the Kentish king Aethelberht looked with suspicion upon St Augustine and his fellow missionaries, and received them in the open air, taking care 'that they should not come to him in any house, lest by so coming, according to an ancient superstition, if they practised any magical art, they might get the better of him and so deceive him'. When the original Latin of this passage was turned into Old English the translator gave it a different turn of meaning, for he reported that Aethelberht, by sitting in the open air, 'employed an ancient countercharm' to prevent himself from being bewitched by the strange incomers. Another story told by Bede, that of the thane Imma, compares Christian and non-Christian magic. After a battle between Northumbrians and Mercians Imma had been taken prisoner, but the fetters put upon him kept falling off again. His captors were baffled, and asked him if he had about him any 'releasing letters' (*litteras solutorias*, whatever that may mean), which would prevent them binding him. But this was not the cause of Imma's release. The thane's brother, abbot Tunna, believed him dead, and kept saying masses for his soul. At every celebration Imma's bonds were loosed. Bede here shows the power of Christianity, but the people who took part in the story were thinking of something different, something more primitive, apparently a magical formula written on parchment or some object bearing magical letters.

Clearly both paganism and magic involved traffic with evil forces, so later Anglo-Saxon writers do not distinguish between heathendom and such varied activities as witchcraft, lot-casting, divination and magic proper. All are condemned together. The penitential of Theodore proscribes in turn sacrifice to demons, the practices of placing children upon a roof or in an oven to heal fever, and of burning grain after a death 'for the health of the living and of the house', incantations and divinations, and the eating of sacrificial food, and to these other penitentials add augury from the flight of birds, observations of the moon's eclipses, lot-casting, making *ligaturas* (that is, strips of inscribed parchment bound round various parts of the body), observing dreams, herbs and so on. Despite this type of attack, magic continued to be used in Anglo-Saxon England, partly because the people of the time had no real way of distinguishing it from science. Thus, much medicine was magic, and magic was used too for many of the daily processes of life.

As a consequence quite a large number of charms survive in Anglo-Saxon manuscripts. These are often in medical texts such as the *Leechbook*, which has a note to say that it (or perhaps its exemplar) was owned by a man called Bald, presumably a professional doctor. Other charms survive in a more chancy way, on the fly-leaves or in the margins of books devoted to other material. To take one example, the margins of a manuscript of the Old English Bede which came into the Exeter library contain charms against eye trouble and the ferocities of all demons, charms to help childbirth, to recover stolen cattle and to catch a swarm of bees, as well as homilies, religious material and an Old English poem on the *paternoster*. Charms vary in form, sometimes preserving only the incantation, while at others there are complicated though imprecise receipts for salves, physics and potions. Surviving charms are predominantly medical, obstetrical and veterinary, and indeed that is why they have survived, because they preserve practical

Anglo-Saxon charm for catching a swarm of bees

methods of dealing with everyday catastrophes. But also they cover quite a wide range of other activities, including finding thieves, ensuring protection on journeys and against witches, elves, dwarfs and other doubtful creatures, increasing the fertility of fields and gaining favours from one's superior.

As an example of an Anglo-Saxon charm giving both actions to be done and words to be chanted, I quote one used to prevent the loss of a swarm of bees, a valuable commodity for the farmer since honey was the only sweetening stuff known and was the main ingredient of mead. The instructions are:

Take some earth and throw it up with your right hand, and so beneath your right foot, and recite,

I catch it under my foot; I have found it.
Lo! earth has power over all creatures,
And against envy and against forgetfulness
And against the mighty tongue of man.

And then, when they swarm, throw sand over them and recite,

Settle, women of victory, sink to the ground,
Never fly wild to the wood,
Be as mindful of my advantage
As every man is of food and land.

Here are two actions, each with its verse. The first shows the magician recognising the mighty powers of earth, yet controlling them by treading earth beneath his foot. Thus he gains over all creatures power which will be used when the bees swarm. During the swarming he employs sympathetic magic, making the mass of bees sink to the ground as the grains of sand fall.

38

At the same time his action may be practical, for the sand may break the speed of flight and make the bees settle the sooner and the nearer.

The Anglo-Saxon charms use types of magic familiar from other civilisations. Some employ number magic, three and its multiples being favourites. To cure dysentery the practitioner must cut nine bramble chips, sing *miserere me deus* three times and nine *paternosters*, boil the chips in milk with two other ingredients and use the result as a potion, three doses of which is guaranteed efficacious. Other charms involve carrying out the actions in silence, or at particular times of day, especially dawn or sunset, or with materials of stated colours, or specifically with the right or left hand. There are many different ingredients: herbs, water, ale, wine, honey, sweat, spittle, excrements, iron. Some spells require the repetition of passages of gibberish, *ecce dol gola ne dit dudum bethe cunda bræthe cunda elecunda* and so on. The gibberish may contain words from other languages, Greek, Hebrew, Celtic, embedded within it and obviously no longer meaningful. Often the words to be spoken have scriptural reference— +*crux Mattheus* +*crux Marcus* +*crux Lucas* +*crux Iohannes* or *Cristus natus aaius* [*agios*] *sanctus*. Sometimes there is a clear and open mixture of Christian and pre-Christian elements. The bee-charm already quoted is probably pagan in origin though it is not openly so, yet it was preserved in a Christian community.

A more curious mixture still is a charm used 'to improve your fields if they will not grow well or if any wicked thing has been done to them by sorcery or witchcraft'. The ceremony takes a whole day, beginning before daybreak and ending before sunset. The performer cuts four turf sods from four parts of the field, concocts a potion of oil, honey, yeast, milk, parts of trees and herbs and holy water, and drips it three times on the undersides of the turfs. Then he carries them to church and has the priest sing four masses over them. He cuts four crosses of aspen, writes on them the names of the evangelists, puts them into the holes the turfs are cut from, and replaces the sods. At various times throughout he must recite chants, partly Latin, partly English, part in verse, part derived from the liturgy, while he must also bow nine times to the east, and turn three times with the course of the sun. Thereafter he takes unknown seed from beggars, repaying them two-fold, collects the ploughing implements together, and puts magical potions and seed in the plough, repeating a partly heathen charm which begins:

Erce, Erce, Erce, mother of earth,
May the almighty eternal lord grant thee
Fields growing and springing,
Fruitful and strength-giving. . . .

A later verse in the charm begins with an invocation curiously parallel to the *ave Maria*: 'Hail to thee, earth, mother of men'. While this is spoken the plough cuts the first furrow, beneath which a loaf is put and then a hymn is chanted to God who made these lands. The ceremony ends with *crescite, in nomine patris sitis benedicti* and *amen* repeated three times, and three *paternosters*.

A charm against dysentery preserves details of one of the *ligaturae* which the church so disdained. The instructions are: 'Write this on a piece of parchment long enough to encircle the head, and hang it round the neck of the man who needs it'. The formula itself is gibberish, comprising words in Hebrew, Aramaic, Latin and Greek, together with meaningless letter groups. Despite the church's strictures, it ends with *alpha* and *omega* and *alleluiah*. The Anglo-Saxons certainly carried such inscribed amulets against sickness or danger, as a group of three related rings demonstrates. These, one unprovenanced and the others from Bramham Moor, Yorkshire, and

Runic amulet rings

Greymoor Hill, Cumberland, have texts in the characters called runes which some scholars believe were developed primarily for magical purposes. Bramham Moor and Greymoor Hill are both in the noble metal gold, and have closely related texts consisting of 30 letters. On Bramham Moor these are disposed outside the hoop, divided by decorative symbols into groups of nine, nine and 12. In the case of Greymoor Hill, 27 are cut outside the hoop, the other three inside it. The text reads *ærkriufltkriuri-*

þonglæstæpontol, at first sight meaningless, but the beginning, *ærkriu*, is clearly related to the sequence *ærcrio* found in some written charms for stanching blood, and there are other resemblances, too, to the gibberish of the manuscript charms. Thus these rings are inscribed with magical formulae whose power is perhaps enhanced by number magic—multiples of three in the letter groupings. The rings date from the ninth century and, being of gold, belonged to people of some wealth. However strongly the church inveighed against such things, people of quality continued to use them.

There are other objects identified as amulets, found in graves from as late as the eighth century, though this time they are uninscribed and the identification is less secure. Natural objects such as pieces of amber, amethyst, rock crystal, agate, chalk, lignite, pebbles and fossils are laid in the burials (usually those of women) in such a way as to suggest they had particular importance. At Eriswell, Cambridgeshire, for instance, a piece of iron-stone, carefully wrapped in a fine linen cloth, was put beneath the dead woman's head.

A people which believed in the efficacy of such amulets was also a people which anticipated attack which it did not understand, attack perhaps from evil demons or from those evil men or women who were in league with them. Certainly the Anglo-Saxons had this fear. The anti-rheumatism charm mentioned above is prescribed as a remedy against the shot of *esa* (a genitive plural; the word is cognate with the Old Norse *Æsir*, 'heathen gods') or the shot of elves or the shot of witches. Witchcraft is often defined and castigated in the laws and church canons, linked with heathendom, idolatry, necromancy, lot-casting and murderous sorcery, though we cannot be sure how much of this reflects genuine belief, and how much derives from non-Anglo-Saxon sources. There are condemnations of 'women who customarily receive enchanters, magicians and witches' and those who 'practise witchcraft dealing with a man's love' or who give him philtres to increase his affection. The most celebrated reference to Anglo-Saxon witchcraft occurs in a tenth-century charter recording an exchange of lands between bishop Aethelwold of Winchester and one

Sorcerer sorcering

Wulfstan Ucca. Defining how Wulfstan came to own one of his estates, the charter says: 'And a widow and her son had previously forfeited the land at Ailsworth because they drove an iron pin into Aelfsige, Wulfstan's father. And it was detected, and the murderous instrument [the Old English word is *morth*, which means 'death, homicide'] dragged from her chamber. And the woman was seized and drowned at London Bridge, but her son escaped and became an outlaw. And the land came into the king's hands, and he gave it to Aelfsige, whose son Wulfstan then gave it to bishop Aethelwold.' This seems a case of a witch sticking pins into the wax image of a man in order to injure him, and the word *morth* presumably applies to the figure. No detail survives of the relationship thought to exist between such a woman and the evil powers she employed, though there is a pregnant reference in one of the charms to 'women with whom the devil has sexual relations'.

Both pagan and Christian Anglo-Saxons, then, lived in a world where superstititon was strong, its effects powerful in everyday life. Outside the inhabited world, in the deserts and waste places, lived monsters and demons. *Beowulf* describes the haunting of a great royal hall by a pair of monsters, mother and son, who lived beneath a neighbouring mere. No clear picture emerges of either, but the son, Grendel, is huge, vicious and bloodthirsty. An evil light shines from his eyes, and weapons cannot harm him. He gulps down the bodies of men. His dam is only less terrible in being female rather than male. Of course, *Beowulf* is a poem, not a history, but it may reflect actual belief. *Grendles mere*, 'Grendel's pond', is recorded once or twice as a

42

place-name. Grendel is called a *thyrs*, a word which survived dialectally until modern times in the form *thurse*, 'goblin', and in the compound *thurse-hole*, 'hollow in a rock or hill where a thurse was thought to live'. According to the Cottonian gnomic verses 'the thurse is a creature living alone, inland in the fen', while place-names preserve the word as in Thirlspott, Cumberland, 'thurse's pit'; Tusmore, Oxfordshire, 'thurse's mere'. Elves too were harmful, though we are not sure what the Anglo-Saxons meant by the word. There are charms against various types of elf-sickness, and against other threats from these beings. The word occurs as a first element of such place-names as Alvedon, Lancashire, 'elf valley'; Elva Hill, Cumberland; and Eldon, Derbyshire, 'elf hill', an area which has a huge pothole where perhaps the elves lived. Place-name material again is our main source of information on other demons, such as the *scucca* and the *scinna*, who haunted such places as Shacklow, Derbyshire, 'demon mound'; Shuckburgh, Warwickshire, 'goblin hill'; Shincliffe, Co. Durham, 'demon cliff'; and Skinburness, Cumberland, 'haunted castle'.

The dragon on the Sutton Hoo shield

The final part of *Beowulf* describes the aging hero's fight against a ferocious fire-breathing dragon, which ravages the country after its hoard of treasure has been plundered from the mound where it lives. This is a common literary motif, but again there is some evidence of parallel folk-belief, as in the place-names Drakelow, Derbyshire, 'dragon's mound'; Drake North, Wiltshire, 'dragon's hoard'. The Cottonian gnomic verses describe the dragon as living 'in a mound, ancient, proud in its treasures'. Sober historical record, too, notes

43

the appearance of dragons in Anglo-Saxon England, though admittedly on special occasions. In 793, according to the *Chronicle*, fiery dragons flew the Northumbrian skies, ominous portents of the coming Viking onslaughts.

The Anglo-Saxons' lack of scientific knowledge, their lack of scientific curiosity even, led them thus into a strange world of superstition, which must often have been a world of terror. Their England was peopled by a large number of creatures which over the years have become extinct. When St Guthlac sought a place of solitude for his hermitage, he picked on the fenland site of Crowland which many had rejected 'because of the unknown portents of the deserts and its terrors of various shapes'. Not surprisingly the cell he built there was soon invaded by hosts of wicked sprites, squeezing in at every cranny and opening. They were 'ferocious in appearance, terrible in shape, with great heads, long necks, thin faces, yellow complexions, filthy beards, shaggy ears, wild foreheads, fierce eyes, foul mouths, horses' teeth, throats vomiting flames, twisted jaws, thick lips, strident voices, singed hair, fat cheeks, pigeon breasts, scabby thighs, knotty knees, crooked legs, swollen ankles, splay feet, spreading mouths and raucous cries.' No Anglo-Saxon would have been surprised at the appearance of such creatures in a place so forbidding and solitary as the fen.

Further Reading

There is no adequate, large-scale account of Anglo-Saxon paganism in English, though a number of articles are important, as Bruce Dickins, 'English Names and Old English Heathenism', *Essays and Studies by Members of the English Association*, vol. XIX, 1933; the same author's 'Place-names formed from Animal-Head Names', in J. E. B. Gover, A. Mawer and F. M. Stenton, *The Place-Names of Surrey*, English Place-Name Society, vol. XI; and F. M. Stenton, 'Anglo-Saxon Heathenism', *Transactions of the Royal Historical Society*, 4th ser., vol. XXIII, 1941. A. L. Meaney, *A Gazetteer of Early Anglo-Saxon Burial Sites*, summarises finds and funeral customs from many sites. G. R. Storms, *Anglo-Saxon Magic*, is an anthology of texts in both original and translation, with an extensive introduction. The Scandinavian material can be seen in H. R. E. Davidson, *Gods and Myths of Northern Europe*.

IV

King and Commoner, Earl and Churl

Anglo-Saxon society was hierarchical: its ranks were king, thane (or *gesith*), churl and slave. There is nothing peculiarly Anglo-Saxon about this social order, which presumably derives from Germanic times. Generalising about that society in his *Germania*, Tacitus described the privileged position of the king or chief, and the relationship between him and his subjects: 'On the field of battle it is a disgrace to the chief to be surpassed in valour by his companions, to the companions not to come up to the valour of their chief. As for leaving a battle alive after your chief has fallen, that means lifelong infamy and shame. To defend and protect him, to put down one's own acts of heroism to his credit—that is what they really mean by "allegiance". The chiefs fight for victory, the companions for their chief.'

The earliest recorded invaders of England attacked under the leadership of their kings or chiefs, Hengest and Horsa in Kent, Aelle and his three sons Cymen, Wlencing and Cissa in Sussex, and Cerdic and his son Cynric in the area which was to become Wessex. There must have been many minor kings too, such as the Haesta whose people, the *Hæstingas*, gave their name to Hastings. By 600, after a century and a half of sporadic warfare and settlement, there were 10 kingdoms south of the Humber, though in some cases we have no regnal lists for them: Kent, Sussex, Wessex, Essex, East Anglia, Lindsey, Mercia, Middle Anglia and the kingdoms of the *Magonsætan* and the *Hwicce* who occupied the two banks of the Severn. North of the

45

Humber developed the territories of Deira and Bernicia. With the passage of years the number of individual kingdoms declined as they coalesced into larger units, Northumbria, Mercia, Wessex, Kent and East Anglia, and ultimately the descendants of the West Saxon house became kings of all England.

The royal families were proud of their origins, keeping their genealogies carefully back as far as the great gods Woden or Seaxnet. The word 'king', Old English *cyning*, means 'man of family', and the members of the family indicated their kinship by the use of personal names which alliterated with one another or which had one element in common—for example, the names of the early East Saxon kings began with the letter *s*, as Saeberht, Sexred, Saeweard, Sigeberht, Sighere, while Alfred the Great's brothers were called Aethelbald, Aethelberht, Aethelred, all the sons of Aethelwulf. Family pride is recorded in the genealogies repeated in the historical sources, and the Old English poem on the *Battle of Brunanburh* tells how king Athelstan and prince Edmund 'cut through the shield-wall, hacked the lime-wood with their hammered swords, as it was natural to men of their ancestry to defend in frequent battles their land, treasure and homes from all enemies'. Often a dynasty took its name from an early and distinguished member, as the East Anglian Wuffingas traced their descent from one Wuffa; in turn Wuffa probably traced his descent from Sweden since the great royal treasure found in the burial-ship of Sutton Hoo contained heirlooms of Swedish origin.

The early kings probably had religious functions as did those of Scandinavia, and a few surviving early royal objects point to this more mystical or formal aspect of kingship. From Sutton Hoo, for example, is a great unwieldy whetstone, neither meant for practical use nor ever used. Its ends are decorated with carved human heads, painted and encaged in bronze frames. This was a ceremonial object, though we do not know its significance. Scholars have suggested severally that it shows a royal cult of the god Thunor, or that it represents the king as the giver of swords and so as leader of battles. The richly decorated helmet from the same site may have been the head-dress symbolic of royalty, predecessor of the crown. Also from

Ceremonial whetstone from Sutton Hoo

46

Sutton Hoo is a curious iron frame upon a staff, the whole surmounted by the figure of a stag or hart, which is thought to have been a royal symbol. This object has been called a standard and linked to the golden banner which the retainers of the dead king Scyld set over his body in the first episode of *Beowulf*. More cogent

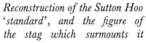

Reconstruction of the Sutton Hoo 'standard', and the figure of the stag which surmounts it

is the parallel with the pomp of the seventh-century Northumbrian king Edwin, who imposed his authority upon other Anglo-Saxon and Celtic peoples. 'So great was his majesty that his standards were borne before him not only in battle; in peace-time too, when he was riding through his cities, towns and provinces, his standard-bearer used to go in front. Also, wherever he walked through the streets the sort of standard which the Romans called *tufa* and the English *thuuf* was carried before him.' Something of this same sense of dignity, a striving after an imperial effect, may have encouraged some Anglo-Saxon kings to model their coins on imperial Roman prototypes.

In the little heroic literature which survives, the king plays an imposing role, the centre-point of a court which had state and etiquette. In *Beowulf* the aged Hrothgar feasts in his great ceremonial hall, listens to the minstrel's song and bestows treasures. When the stranger Beowulf arrives he is formally received by the herald Wulfgar, who takes his message to the king; of Wulfgar the poet comments, 'he knew the etiquette appropriate to an experienced courtier'. The king

47

receives the newcomers with ceremony, seats them in his hall where a cupbearer serves them, and where later they are welcomed by Wealhtheow, Hrothgar's queen. After Beowulf has vanquished the monster Grendel, he is feasted and rewarded, given among other presents a great golden collar. This quality of generosity in a king is a popular literary motif. 'A king's duty is to give rings in the hall', says one of the Cottonian gnomic verses. The king is called *sincgifa* or *maththumgyfa*, 'treasure-giver', *beaga brytta*, 'distributor of rings', *goldwine gumena*, 'gold-friend of men', and again the gnomic verses say pointedly: 'It is the duty of good *gesithas* (retainers) to urge a young prince on to battle and to ring-giving.' This liberality binds the king to his immediate followers, encouraging them to support him at need. The relationship goes back to Germanic times: 'The companions are prodigal in their demands on the generosity of their chiefs', says Tacitus. From the ninth century survive two gold finger-rings engraved with the names and titles of *Aethelwulf rex* and *Aethelswith regina*, plausibly identified with the father and sister of Alfred the Great. These may have been designed as gifts to be handed over at formal ceremonies to favoured courtiers. Miss V. I. Evison has ingeniously suggested that the rings sometimes added to early sword hilts may symbolise this same king–courtier relationship.

The formal aspect of kingship was not solely a literary convention. Historical sources make clear that some Anglo-Saxon kings held considerable state. The opening of a charter of 970 refers thus to the collaboration between king Edgar and the Almighty: 'I Edgar, exalted as king over the English nation by His grace, as He has now reduced beneath my sway Scots and Cumbrians and likewise Britons and all that this island contains, so that I now occupy my throne in peace . . .' From such wording it is easy to believe Florence of Worcester's story of

King Aethelwulf's ring

this king's splendid consecration in 973. His eight sub-kings rowed him from his palace at Chester to the monastery of St John the Baptist, accompanied by a fleet of boats for his nobles. Edgar spoke of the pride any of his successors might feel at 'being king of the English, when he might have the glory of such honours, with so many kings subservient to him'. The Bayeux tapestry, for what it is worth as evidence, shows Edward the Confessor seated in state upon his ornamented

King Edgar and the Almighty

throne, wearing a crown and holding his sceptre.

The king, then, occupied a position pre-eminent in dignity, in rank and also in law. Inevitably he carried the responsibilities of such an office. Some of these were administrative, particularly in the later period as the details of government became more and more complex, for instance in the business of organising the royal coinage. Some were military—*Beowulf* describes the great Scyld as a good king because 'he flourished in honours until each of the neighbouring peoples across the sea came under his authority, paid him tribute'. This aspect of kingship covered the whole of the Anglo-Saxon period. The early kings, of whom little is known but their names, were war-leaders, while the last Anglo-Saxon king fell amidst his bodyguard on the field of battle, defending his throne against the invader. But there were moral duties too, specifically expressed in the Christian writings of later Anglo-Saxon times. The Old English preface to the

49

translation of Bede's *Ecclesiastical History* contains the comment: 'Because God chose you as king, it behoves you to teach your people', an admonition which king Alfred, who inspired the work, well heeded. Archbishop Wulfstan of York compiled his *Institutes of Polity* in the early eleventh century, during the irresolute and irresponsible reign of Aethelred the Unready. His description of the ideal king stands in sharp contrast to contemporary practice: 'For a Christian king it is most appropriate that he should govern a Christian people justly, and that he should be, as is right, the consolation of his people and a good shepherd of a Christian flock.' He must extend Christianity, support and protect the church, bring his people to peace by just laws, and encourage the good while punishing the wicked with severity; that is, he must be the *rex justus* of Christian teaching. The contemporary annalist saw these qualities in the sainted Edward the Confessor, whose death he mourned in a verse passage of the *Chronicle*. He remembered Edward as a gracious ruler, one free from sin, pure and gentle, strong in counsels, who dispensed wealth, ruled the Welsh, Scots and Britons as well as the English, a noble prince who defended his fatherland, realm and people.

Linked to his rise in moral status is the church's recognition of the king's position. In Germanic societies the monarchy was traditionally elective. The man chosen would be 'throneworthy' because of his membership of the royal family but, theoretically at any rate, the people picked from that family

Edward the Confessor sits in state

A great man's charity

the man most suitable to reign. The later Anglo-Saxon church added consecration to election. The first example, as far as our records go, was Ecgferth, son of Offa of Mercia, consecrated in 787 while his father was still living. Thereafter the practice may rapidly have become common, for the *Chronicle* tells that in 796 Eardwulf of Northumbria was enthroned in the presence of archbishop Eanbald and the bishops of Hexham, Lindisfarne and Whithorn. Later the ceremony included a royal oath. That of Aethelred the Unready, which survives to us, contains the threefold promise that there should be peace within the church and among all his people, that robbery and other forms of injustice should cease, and that his judgments should be based on justice and mercy.

The church's recognition of the institution of kingship led to developments in political thought. The king was defined as 'Christ's deputy among Christian people' who 'must avenge very

Harold crowned king. Archbishop Stigand stands beside him

zealously offences against Christ'. As Christ's deputy he could not be expelled from his office. He rules, as the charters attest, 'by the help of God', 'by the grant of the most omnipotent Lord', 'by the favour of the divine grace', 'by the abundant grace of God and the gratuitous gift of him who thunders and rules', and Cnut's laws record his recognition of 'the power that it has pleased God to give me'. The king's position in law was traditionally strong. Crimes, fighting and drawing weapons, in his presence were heavily punished. Breach of the king's peace, given with his own hand, could not be compensated for. A deserter from the army led by the king could suffer loss of life and property, but the offence entailed only a fine of 120 shillings if the king were not present. To a privileged position like this the later law-codes add a quality of sanctity. The king's position is ranked, sometimes with that of bishop, sometimes above that of archbishop. In Edmund's code is the decree that no man guilty of bloodshed should enter the royal presence until he had done penance and agreed to make redress for his act. Aethelred's fifth code, in which archbishop Wulfstan had a great hand, forbids any excommunicated man to stay in the king's neighbourhood until he has submitted to ecclesiastical penance. The pagan war-chief of early times has developed into the Christian leader of a Christian people.

A Christian king: Cnut crowned by an angel

52

Below the king in dignity came the freemen. There were several ranks of them, their numbers and individual titles varying with time and place. For the moment—and as a generalisation—it is convenient to divide the freemen into two groups defined by their social positions rather than their functions. There was an upper group of noblemen variously called earls, *gesithas* or thanes, while a lower group of common freemen or churls (*ceorlas*) made up the main body of the Anglo-Saxon people. These two groups had rights and obligations in common. They were liable to taxation and church dues, could be called upon for military service, and had the duty of attendance at legal assemblies. In return they had privileges, of owning land, of freedom to move from one part of the country to another, and a fixed measure of protection from the law. The difference between these classes was largely one of wealth. The *Rectitudines singularum personarum*, an eleventh-century document on the rights and duties of individuals, defines the thane's position as to be 'entitled to his book-right [that is, land held on the evidence of a charter, disposable at will and free from most obligations], and that he shall contribute three things in respect of his land, armed service, and the repairing of fortresses, and work on bridges'. A thane's book-land might comprise large estates scattered over the country, on which he lived, progressing from one to another throughout the year. Wulfric Spott was a Mercian thane related to the royal house of that province. By his will, compiled in the early eleventh century, he left estates in at least nine counties of the north and Midlands to a large number of people, to archbishop Aelfric, to his brother Aelfhelm and nephew Wulfheah, to his daughter, his god-daughter and a number of retainers and kinsmen. Of course, this was a man of exceptional wealth. Perhaps more typical is ealdorman Alfred, whose will, drawn up between 871 and 888, disposes of land in Kent and Surrey. To his widow, daughter, illegitimate son and kinsmen he left over 100 hides of land. A hide is the measure of land enough theoretically to support a single household. This seems in origin to have been the churl's holding over much of the country, though some owned more than this, and some, particularly in the later period, less. Evidence suggests that the maximum holding for a churl was five hides. An early eleventh-century compilation of traditions regarding social ranks and status, looking back to the good old days, comments, 'and if a churl prospered so that he owned fully five hides of land of his own, a bell and a castle-gate, a seat and special office in the king's hall, then he was henceforth entitled to the rights of a thane', while the *Law of the North People*, recorded from the same date, also sets the possession of five hides of land as a minimum requirement for raising a churl's status, 'and even if he prospers so that he owns a helmet and mail-coat and a gold-plated sword, if he has not got the land he is a churl just the same'. There was, then, some mobility between these social groups, though a limited one, for the rules demanded continued success over three generations before the raised status became hereditary: 'And if his son and his son's son prosper so that they have that much land, then the offspring is of *gesith*-born class.'

Though these definitions are generally correct, they were subject to many local variations. The *Rectitudines* remind us that customs vary from one estate to the next, and from our different sources we are constantly meeting references to social groups which do not fit the simple picture. Some men of the *gesith* class were landless, perhaps young people who had not yet been given estates, and who lived in the households of wealthy nobles or who rented land. The same applied to some churls. Thus we have the situation which king Alfred illustrated in his preface to the translation of St Augustine's *Soliloquies*: 'But, when a man has built a manor on land leased from his lord and with his lord's help, he likes to stay on it from time to time, hunting, fowling and fishing, and supporting himself in all sorts of ways, by land and sea, on that leased property, until by his lord's grace he can acquire bookland and a perpetual inheritance'. There were grades of freeman below the churl— manumitted slaves, Celts of various ranks. Some estates had paid workers. Some freemen lived outside the agricultural system, like the merchant mentioned in an eleventh-century tract, who, by virtue of having travelled overseas at his own expense on three occasions, was entitled to a thane's privileges.

The *Rectitudines* lists numbers of people whose freedom is restricted in various ways: the thane who holds an estate in respect of such services as equipping a guard ship for the king, or keeping military watch, or the *geneat*, a man of some standing, who must pay rent, and act on behalf of his lord, carrying his messages, guarding him, looking to the horses, and keeping up hides from which he could shoot deer.

So far I have omitted a most important aspect of this hierarchical system of king, thane and churl. A man's social position was defined by his *wergild*. This is a legal term whose literal meaning is 'man-payment' or 'man-tax'. It represents a man's financial value in law, the fine payable if he is killed. *Wergild* regulations were different in different parts of the country, but general principles apply. The laws of the kings Hlothhere and Eadric of Kent, who ruled in the 670s and 680s, mention the *eorlcund* man, of noble rank, who has a *wergild* of 300 shillings (6,000 pence at the Kentish rate of twenty to the shilling), and the freeman of 100 shillings (2,000 pence) *wergild*. The laws of king Alfred of Wessex, in the late ninth century, mention three ranks, with *wergilds* of 1,200 shillings (6,000 pence at the West Saxon rate of five to the shilling), 600 shillings (3,000 pence) and 200 shillings (1,000 pence). The first two of these are of noble rank (though other sources give little about the 600-shilling man, who was presumably rare), while the third is the churl whose value with respect to the nobleman is thus only half that of his Kentish counterpart. The king was fitted into this system, having his own, enormous, *wergild*.

The Alfred jewel, traditionally associated with Alfred the Great. It bears the text +AELFRED MEC HEHT GEWYRCAN, '*Alfred had me made*'

According to the *Law of the North People* this was 30,000 *thrymsas* or 90,000 pence, half of which was the king's personal *wergild*, half belonging to the royal office. The *Law of the Mercians* gives the king's simple *wergild* as six times that of a thane, namely 7,200 shillings (at the Mercian rate of four pence to the shilling), with an equal amount pertaining to the office.

The primary purpose of the *wergild* system was to fix the size of compensation to be paid to the kinsmen of a slain man. It had other uses too, for it regulated many forms of legal recompense. For example, according to Alfred's laws, a man who committed adultery with the wife of a 1200-man had to pay him 120 shillings; the same offence with the wife of a 600-man cost 100 shillings; with the wife of a churl 40 shillings. The fine for forced entry into a house varied from 120 shillings in the case of the king's hall to five shillings for a churl's cottage. Higher social rank implied higher responsibility before the law. If a woman who was betrothed committed fornication she had to pay to her surety 120 shillings if she was of the 1200-man class, but only 60 shillings if she was *ceorl*-born. The laws of Ine of Wessex fixed the fines for neglect of military service at 120 shillings (and forfeiture of land) for the land-owning *gesith*, half that sum for a *gesith* who owned no land, 30 shillings for a *ceorl*. By Alfred's laws a thief who stole from a church might have his hand struck off. If he were allowed to keep it, he might redeem it at a price proportionate to his *wergild*. There were compensating legal advantages. In their law-suits the Anglo-Saxons were little concerned with investigating guilt or establishing right and wrong. A case usually involved the confrontation of plaintiff and defendant, and the procedure allowed the defendant to assert his innocence by swearing an oath to that effect, helped by compurgators who were willing to confirm his oath. The oath of a nobleman was more highly respected than that of a churl. In Mercia, we are told, that of a 1200-man was worth the oath of six *ceorls*. The treaty between Alfred and Guthrum provides that a king's thane accused of manslaughter could clear himself by the oaths of 12 king's thanes. A man of lower rank required only 11

56

of his equals together with one king's thane to swear to his innocence.

The bonds which held these different social classes together were those of loyalty and mutual dependence. The king surrounded himself with his retainers, who served him and pledged loyalty. In the vernacular literature these courtiers are divided into two groups, the *duguth*, the older, tried men who presumably had estates of their own and so lived with the king only intermittently, and the *geoguth*, the young warriors who attended the king in the hope of rewards of treasure, office or land. The historical sources confirm this division. In the same way the great secular lords had beneath them men of lower rank or lesser wealth, who supported them and expected help in return.

The relationship between lord and man was a voluntary one, for with permission a freeman could leave serving one lord and move to another. But the relationship was also a formal one, and must have been recorded in some public contract or ceremony. A man's lord had a legal position. By the laws of Ine he was entitled to compensation for the death of one of his men, over and above the *wergild* payable to the kinsmen. In Athelstan's code a lord who failed to bring to justice one of his men guilty of theft must repay the value of the stolen goods and was liable to a fine from the king. The lord was expected to support his man in difficulty and danger, and sometimes did it too fervently, for Cnut complained that 'many an overbearing man will, if he can and may, defend his man whichever way he thinks he can defend him more easily, whether as a freeman or a slave; but this abuse we will not allow.' He must also be a generous lord, rewarding his man with gifts and privileges. In return the man helps his lord, fights at his side and if need be dies in avenging him.

Much vernacular Anglo-Saxon literature is devoted to celebrating the lord–man relationship, dwelling on the generosity of the lord and the loyalty of the retainer. The sentiments— recorded as early as Tacitus—are heroic ones, and find their most elaborate expression in heroic poems such as *Beowulf* and *The Fight at Finnesburh*. They survive even as late as the disastrous reign of Aethelred the Unready. The *Chronicle* records that, in 991, a Viking fleet under one Olaf attacked East Anglia, reaching Maldon in Essex: 'And ealdorman Byrhtnoth came to meet them there with his levies and fought them, but they killed the ealdorman there and had control of the battle-field.' Shortly after this mêlée an unknown Englishman wrote a poem of marked power, celebrating the valour of Byrhtnoth and his followers' faithfulness to death. Byrhtnoth is loyal to *his* lord, the king, rejecting with savage irony the pirates' demand to be bought off, and announcing: 'Here amidst his army stands a noble warrior who intends to defend this country, the home, people and land of my prince Aethelred.' When a Viking wounds the ealdorman with a javelin, Wulfmaer, a young retainer, avenges him by pulling the weapon from the wound and throwing it back, killing the assailant. After Byrhtnoth's death in battle, some of his levies flee, to the poet's disgust. His retainers stand firm, remembering promises made to their lord when they lived at ease in his hall. The poem ends with the formal speeches made by these heroic fighters as they advance, determined either to avenge their leader or lie in death beside him. 'Leofsunu spoke, raising his linden shield in defence . . . . "I vow that I shall not retreat a foot's space from here. Instead I shall advance, avenging my dear lord in the struggle. Though my lord has fallen, the sturdy warriors of Sturmer will have no occasion to mock me for returning home leaderless or fleeing from battle. Weapon shall take me, spear-point or iron blade".'

Byrhtnoth commanded the loyalty of men of various classes. Dunnere is a 'simple churl', who calls laconically upon his comrades to fight on: 'A man intent on avenging his lord on this army must not waver or worry about his life.' Even a Northum-

The fight round king Harold at Hastings

brian hostage who was being lodged with Byrhtnoth shoots with bow and arrow until he is cut down. Classic among the quotations from Old English literature is the speech of Byrht-wold, an old member of the ealdorman's household: 'As our might declines, the more resolute must be our temper, the bolder our hearts, the greater our spirits. Here on the sand lies our leader, cut down. Those who turn away from battle now will regret it for ever. I am an old man, I will not leave, for I intend to lie by my chief's side, beside so dear a man.'

There are enough parallel examples from historical sources to show that these speeches are not mere bombast. The body-guards of Theodbald of the royal house of Northumbria, and of the contesting princes Cyneheard and Cynewulf of Wessex fell with their lords, and there are many cases of individual heroism in men defending or avenging their superiors. The *Chronicle*, annal 755, records that Sigeberht, deposed king of Wessex, was driven from Hampshire, his last stronghold in the kingdom, when he killed ealdorman Cumbra. He fled to the Weald where he was stabbed to death by a swineherd, who thus avenged the ealdorman. Bede tells how, under cover of deliver-ing a message, a West Saxon assassin stabbed at Edwin of Northumbria with a poisoned dagger. Lilla, one of Edwin's thanes, anticipated the attack, but had no shield to protect the king with. So he jumped in front of him, and was killed in-stantly. Retainers were expected to accompany their lord into exile, and many in fact did. Aldhelm of Malmesbury, writing to the clergy who owed allegiance to the exiled bishop, St Wilfrid, compared their case to that of the men of a banished lord: 'If laymen . . . abandon the faithful lord they have loved in prosperity, and, when good fortune is at an end and ill-luck has come upon him, prefer the safe ease of their sweet native land to the afflictions of their exiled chief, does not everyone think they deserve ridicule, horrible jeering and shouts of execration? What then will be said of you if you let the prelate who has fostered and raised you go into exile alone?'

The law recognised the loyal bond between man and lord. Alfred's code, for instance, has the provision: 'A man may fight on behalf of his lord if the latter is attacked, without incurring the blood-feud. Similarly the lord may fight on his man's behalf.' There is a further, related, clause: 'In the same way, a man may fight on behalf of his born kinsman if he is wrongfully attacked, except against his lord. That we do not allow.' This introduces the second type of loyalty which influenced the Anglo-Saxon freeman's life, a loyalty to his family which might reinforce that felt towards his lord, or which might conflict with it. Again, kin-loyalty is a traditional Germanic concept, recorded by Tacitus and found too, for example, among the medieval Scandinavians. The family was a tight-knit unit for defence or offence. Each freeman had his *wergild*, the price to be paid if he were killed. It was the family's duty to exact this compensation, or to take vengeance. Similarly it was up to the killer's family to band together in his defence, perhaps by contributing towards the payment. They could refuse, but in doing so they gave up subsequent claims upon him, must not help him with food or protection, nor could they themselves require *wergild* if he were slain.

The legal codes prescribe how, in practical terms, *wergild* was to be paid, though they build upon customary practice and leave much detail unaccounted for. Some of them are clear attempts to avoid unnecessary bloodshed by formalising practices. By Alfred's laws a man fleeing from a feud who got to a church could have seven days' sanctuary, though no food should be given him during that time. If he handed out his weapons, his pursuers must keep him for 30 days and inform his kin, who would presumably negotiate a settlement. An avenger who caught his opponent at home must demand justice before he attacked, and there are rules about the way an attack could be mounted. Edmund's second code is concerned with preventing the many distressing 'illegal conflicts which take place among us'. Under it the avengers could attack only the killer himself, not members of his family or household. It allowed the offender the sanctuary of church or royal residence. If he were willing to pay the *wergild* he chose a middleman who would approach the dead man's kinsmen with his pledge to pay up. The kinsmen could then give the killer a safe conduct so that he could meet them to offer his pledge in person, finding a surety for the money. After this he was under the king's protection. Within three weeks he must give that proportion of the *wergild* which went to the nearest relatives, and thereafter, at three-week intervals, the lord's compensation for the loss of his man, and the first instalment of the *wergild* proper. The whole debt was due within a twelvemonth.

The blood-feud was a primitive Germanic method of establishing justice between social groups, with the kin having the right, if they wished, to pursue to his death a killer or the members of his family. The amending legislation of the Anglo-Saxons tried to mitigate these disputes, and to introduce to them some elements of Christian forgiveness and practical control while allowing family pride its proper expression. Certainly, we see the Anglo-Saxon family most clearly in its relationship to the feud, but it must have had many other functions affecting the welfare of individual members. They must have helped one another in physical danger or distress, in time of dearth or plague; they watched over the marriage contracts of the women members, being prepared to support them against wrongdoing or accusation if they removed from their own district; they arranged for orphans to be fostered and their property guarded.

I have described here an organic society, in which a man knew his place and had appropriate rights and duties, and in which privileges and responsibilities were related to social rank. The importance of this social thinking is seen in archbishop Wulfstan's accusations given in a sermon preached to the English people 'when the Danes were persecuting them most', that is in 1014. Wulfstan believed the end of the world was nigh, and quoted as his evidence the decline of social awareness, the breaking of the bonds of society: 'Very often now a kinsman protects a kinsman no more than he would a stranger, nor a father his child, nor sometimes a child his own father, nor a man his brother. . . . And there is also very great treachery in this world in a man betraying his lord to death, or driving him living from the land. And both have happened in this country. . . . We know perfectly well, too, where that shame has been committed of a father selling his child for money, and a child his mother, and a man his brother into the hands of strangers.' Such wickedness, thought Wulfstan, had led God to punish the English by unleashing the Vikings upon them. In a similar way some Anglo-Saxon poets stress the social bonds by describing the misery of those who are lordless or kinless. *The Wanderer* is about exile. It shows the man whose lord is dead and whose family is scattered, wandering the earth's surface seeking a new home: 'When sorrow and sleep together often bind the poor solitary wretch, it seems in his fancy that he is embracing and kissing his liege-lord, and laying hands and head upon his knee, as when, in former days, he sometimes enjoyed the throne's bounty. Then the friendless man wakes up again, he sees the tawny waves before him, the seabirds swimming and spreading their wings, frost and snow falling, mingled with hail. Then his heart's wounds are the keener, grieving for his beloved lord. His sorrow is renewed when the memory of his kinsmen passes through his mind.'

The same significant theme, treated more lightly, occurs in one of the Riddles. An Anglo-Saxon riddle takes the form of an ambiguous, often misleading and sometimes very elaborate, description of an object which the hearer is challenged to identify. The answer to Exeter Book Riddle 20 is probably 'a sword'. The riddler portrays it as a warrior fighting in battle: 'I need not expect a son to avenge me on the life of my killer if any foe engages me in battle. The kin from which I descend will not be increased by my children. Unless I, lordless, travel from my owner who gave me rings, I am destined, if I obey my lord and wage war as I always have done at my prince's pleasure, to do without the begetting of children.'

Anglo-Saxon England must have had numbers of men who were kinless or lordless. The man whose family had died out or had disowned him, the man whose lord had died or had dismissed him for some offence, these were vulnerable. It might be hard to find a new lord, for the lord was responsible for his men's crimes, even those committed before he took them on, so a wanderer seeking patronage would be suspect. Some law codes give rights in a stranger's *wergild* and responsibility for his maintenance to the king or the king's reeve. This would give some security, though not comparable with that provided by a strong kin or a powerful lord. The Exeter Book gnomic verses sum up man's situation in the platitudes: 'Wretched is the man who must live alone. Fate has ordained that he shall live friendless. It would be better for him if he had a brother, both the sons of the same warrior. . . . Those men should always bear arms and sleep in company. Never should they be separated in meeting until death part them.'

Towards the end of the period organisations developed to supply some of the functions of family or lord. Cnut required that all free men over 12 years of age should be brought into a hundred or tithing. Only then were they entitled to a free

Manumission records

man's rights of *wergild* and exculpation by oath. Voluntary communities or guilds appear, notably the Cambridge thanes' guild whose regulations survive. They include the provision, 'If anyone kills a guild-brother, nothing less than eight pounds is to be taken in compensation. If the killer scorns to pay compensation, all members of the guild are to avenge the brother, and all must bear responsibility for the feud.'

So far I have spoken of the privileged members of society, the freemen. But Anglo-Saxon England was a slave state. Beneath the freemen were the slaves, different grades of them, and the laws mention other groups of underprivileged people whose exact positions are obscure; for example, the Kentish *læt* who may be a manumitted slave or a subject Celt, the *esne* who is sometimes equated with the slave and sometimes not. In civil law the slave was a piece of property and a working machine, to be bought and sold on the same sort of terms as a horse or as livestock. The will of one Wynflaed, a tenth-century document,

63

records the bequest to her daughter Aethelflaed of an engraved bracelet and brooch, an estate at Ebbesborne, Wiltshire, together with the slaves and stock on it. The slave had no *wergild*, though he had a value—50 or 60 shillings in Ine's laws—which must be paid to his owner if he was killed. His freedom could be bought; a series of manumission records, once in the blank leaves of a gospel book of Bath Abbey, now in manuscripts at Corpus Christi College, Cambridge, witnesses how a number of slaves were freed at various prices such as a pound, half a pound, five shillings, 60 pence, five ores and 12 head of sheep. The slave had few civil rights. Alfred's law-code gives details of one of them: 'The four Wednesdays in the four Ember Weeks are to be given to all slaves, to sell to whoever they choose anything that anyone has given them in God's name, or what they can earn in any of their leisure moments.' From this it is clear that they could own property and money, but in general it is assumed that they were penniless, for, in dealing with criminal slaves, the laws provide for corporal or capital punishment rather than fines. By the time of the *Rectitudines* slaves, at any rate in some parts of the country, had acquired customary privileges. 'A herdsman slave belonging to his lord, who keeps the demesne herd, should have a young pig kept in a sty, and his perquisites when he has prepared the bacon, and also the dues that belong to a slave.' The dues include provisions: '12 lbs of good corn and two carcases of sheep and one good cow for food and the right of cutting wood according to the custom of the estate.'

There were several ways in which an Anglo-Saxon could become a slave. He could be born to the condition, be a prisoner of war or a member of the conquered Celtic peoples, or his family could have sold him into serfdom in time of famine, and indeed have saved him thus from starvation. The type we hear most about in the laws is the penal-slave, who had been found guilty of one of the crimes—theft or incest, for example—for which slavery was a punishment or who had been enslaved because he was too poor to pay the fine for his misdemeanour. Similarly, there were several ways in which an Anglo-Saxon slave could gain his freedom. The simplest was to run away from his master, perhaps joining one of the marauding Viking armies, but absconding was dangerous and punishable by death. He could buy his liberty or have it bought him by relatives. He could be manumitted as an act of grace on his lord's part. In some cases malefactors seem to have been enslaved temporarily, until the product of their labours balanced the sums due in fines or compensations.

Though the church accepted the inequalities of the social system as it affected freemen, it found slavery repugnant and had a good record in encouraging freeing of slaves and suppressing the export trade in them. Anglo-Saxon wills often require slaves to be manumitted as an act of Christian charity. For example, that of Aethelflaed, second wife of king Edmund, stipulates that 'half my men in every village be freed for my soul', while prince Athelstan, leaving his possessions 'to the glory of God and for the redemption of my soul and that of my father King Aethelred', granted first of all 'that every penally enslaved man whom I acquired in the course of jurisdiction be set at liberty'. The slave was not cut off from the mercy of God or of his fellow men, but his existence on large estates was an economic necessity, and his condition must often have been piteous. The ploughman who appears in Aelfric's *Colloquy* describes a back-breaking day's work, and the questioner comments, 'Oh, how toilsome it is.' 'It is great toil, sir,' replies the ploughman, 'because I am not free.'

Further Reading

Dorothy Whitelock, *The Beginnings of English Society*, gives an excellent and well-documented account of social position in Anglo-Saxon England, and the section, 'Government and Society', in her *English Historical Documents*, vol. 1, adds further detail with cross-reference to the primary sources. For the Sutton Hoo material, see R. L. S. Bruce-Mitford, *The Sutton Hoo Ship Burial, a Handbook*. Full translations of the royal legal texts (of which there are extensive selections in *English Historical Documents*) are in F. L. Attenborough, *The Laws of the Earliest English Kings*, and A. J. Robertson, *The Laws of the Kings of England from Edmund to Henry I*. The text of the *Rectitudines* is in *English Historical Documents*, vol. 2.

V

A Woman's Place

'A woman's place is at her embroidery', says a line in the Exeter Book gnomic verses. Such anti-feminism is hardly typical of Anglo-Saxon opinion. Though we see little of the women of Anglo-Saxon England, it is clear that they had considerable freedom, both in law and in practice. Their activities were not confined to kitchen, bower and bed. It is true that Anglo-Saxon poetry often shows woman as a passive creature. In *The Wife's Lament* she suffers hardship, but does little about it. *The Lover's Message* portrays her waiting patiently until she is summoned to join her man. The elegiac and enigmatic *Wulf and Eadwacer* depicts her parted from her lover and mourning him, but doing nothing else. The laconic utterances of the Exeter gnomic verses —'A king shall buy a queen with possessions, with goblets and rings'; 'A woman . . . shall be cheerful, capable of keeping a secret, generous with horses and treasures'; 'A wife must be faithful to her husband'; 'A maid is the joy of her owner'— show her as a secondary figure largely subordinate to the man. Even the lively picture of the sailor's wife in the same text describes her only as she serves her husband: 'Her dear one is a welcome guest to the Frisian woman, when the ship stands at anchor. His boat has docked, and her husband, who supports the family, has come home. She calls him in, washes his sea-stained clothes and gives him fresh ones. On land she grants him what his love desires.'

In the surviving heroic poetry the noble woman plays a decorative part, as a gracious hostess, a generous rewarder of warriors, the central figure of a diplomatic marriage contract which will reconcile warring peoples. For example, Wealhtheow, the Danish queen, appears in the festive intervals of Beowulf's struggles with the monsters, gracefully encouraging that fighter to deeds of valour, praising and rewarding him for his prowess, and encouraging the men of the household to festivity. 'Mindful of court etiquette, Wealhtheow, Hrothgar's queen, came forward. Glittering with gold, the noble woman greeted the men in hall, giving the cup first to the protector of the East Danes. . . . Then the woman of the Helmings [Wealhtheow] went round the warriors, old and young, offering the jewelled cup.' Later she makes a polite speech to Beowulf as he is rewarded for his success by a gift of treasure, including a superb gold collar, and later still, with her daughter Freawaru, she serves the ale-cup to each of the courtiers in turn. Freawaru is to be given in marriage to Ingeld, prince of the Heathobards, in the hope of putting an end to the enmity between them and the Danes, but the poet makes it clear that this hope will be vain.

In the poem *Widsith* also, the queen appears as a ceremonial figure, gold-adorned, distributing gifts to the court-poet. In the Exeter gnomic verses she is partner in generosity to the king: 'Both must primarily be liberal with gifts.' These pictures of the noble lady, though clearly not realistic, are based on fact. In a splendid court like that controlled by Edgar or that implied by the rich royal treasure of Sutton Hoo, the queen may have had such a stately role. As we have seen, queen Aethelswith seems to have been a 'ring-giver', for her name and title occur on an extant gold ring.

In the poetry, too, the noble woman is commonly linked to treasure, jewels, often gold —'A bracelet becomes a bride'; 'Jewelry is proper to a woman'. As parallels we can point to some of the magnificent grave-goods from Anglo-Saxon England. From Desborough, Northamptonshire, comes a seventh-century necklace of gold beads, with gold and garnet pendants and a central gold cross. From Sarre, Kent, there is a necklace of glass beads and amethyst, with four gold coin pendants and a central circular pendant of glass mosaic.

Queen Aethelswith's ring, with her name inscribed behind the bezel

Necklace from Desborough, Northants

Another grave at Sarre produced a mass of treasure, the property
of one wealthy woman: a fragment of gold cloth, a finger-ring
of silver wire, a necklace of six gold bracteates from Scandinavia,
more than 140 beads, most of red amber, which were secured
to the shoulders by a pair of gilt bronze circular brooches
adorned with garnets, shell and glass, two more brooches, one
of silver and one bronze gilt, as well as an elaborate silver spoon
set with garnets, a large ball of rock-crystal, and various more
personal possessions. Some Anglo-Saxon wills show the same
predilection for finery. Wynflaed leaves an engraved ring (the
Old English word is *beag*, which could be a bracelet, arm-ring
or collar) and two brooches, one decorated with filigree, as
well as several silver cups and a wooden one with a gold fitting.
Aelfgifu bequeathes to the queen a necklace, armlet and
drinking-cup, and a headband of some sort to her sister-in-law.
Bede tells how Aethelthryth, who was daughter to king Anna
of East Anglia, wife of king Ecgfrith of Northumbria, and
finally abbess of Ely, suffered in her later years from an abscess
on the jaw. She rejoiced that God gave her this pain, believing

that it would free her from the guilt of her youthful sin of vanity and love of display, 'in that now I bear this burning red tumour on my neck instead of gold and pearls'.

Even in the heroic poetry the woman is not purely a decorative figure, quite inactive in larger matters. While praising Beowulf for his exploits, Wealhtheow seizes the opportunity of asking his help in assuring her sons' future rule, at the same time hinting to her nephew the importance of friendship and loyalty within the family. The queen or noble lady of real life must often have acted a diplomatic part like this, and have been an influence to reckon with. The tenth-century testament of Brihtric and Aelfswith refers to king Edgar's wife in terms which suggest she was a woman worth knowing. After a bequest to the king, it records 'to the queen an armlet of 30 mancuses of gold, and a stallion, for her advocacy that the will might stand'. The diplomatic marriage, linking nations or great families, was common. One of the periphrases for 'woman' in Old English is *freothuwebbe*, 'weaver of peace', and the daughter of a royal house must often have been used to heal enmity between peoples or to cement friendship. Bede shows us one such woman in action. Aethelburh, daughter of the Christian king Aethelberht of Kent, was married to the pagan Edwin of Northumbria. The Pope wrote to her (enclosing a silver mirror and an ivory and gold comb) asking her to use her influence to bring her husband into the church. Certainly Edwin was converted, though whether by his wife's preaching or by that of the missionary Paulinus is not clear.

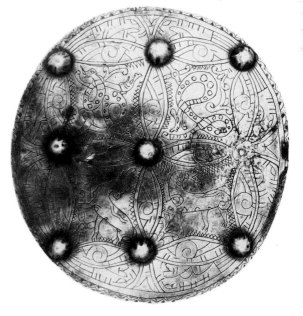

The Sutton, Isle of Ely, brooch. On its back is an inscription recording that it was owned by a woman called Aedwen, and cursing anyone who might steal it

Not all Anglo-Saxon women were content to take this self-effacing attitude. The career of Aethelflaed, called Lady of the Mercians, is instructive. She was the eldest child of Alfred the Great, married to ealdorman Aethelred, ruler of Mercia, in the 880s, and she controlled Mercia, 'holding dominion with lawful authority' for seven years after her husband's death in 911. Indeed, she was probably effective ruler some time earlier, since Aethelred's declining years were spent in sickness and incapacity. Aethelflaed was vigorous and efficient in resisting Viking aggression. Cooperating with her brother, Edward the Elder of Wessex, she built a chain of 10 fortresses against the Midland Danes, at places like Bridgnorth, Tamworth, Stafford and Warwick, and captured the Viking centres of Derby and Leicester. In the north she constructed forts at Chester, Eddisbury and Runcorn, which were to control the Irish–Norwegian immigrant bands who were occupying the Wirral and parts of Cumberland, Westmorland and Lancashire. For a time the people of York recognised her authority, and she concluded anti-Norwegian alliances with the Britons, Picts and Scots. Later sources describe her as directing battle against the Scandinavian Ragnald, and she certainly sent a punitive army into Wales to avenge the killing of abbot Ecgbert and his comrades. She was renowned beyond the bounds of England for the Ulster Annals called her the 'very famous queen of the Saxons'.

An example of an active and respected leader in the religious field is abbess Hild. Born of the royal house of Northumbria, related to that of East Anglia, she spent her first 33 years in the secular life of a noble lady. She was then professed a nun, and settled first on the bank of the Wear where a hide of land was given her to live on. She left to become abbess of Hartlepool, and then moved to *Kælcacæstir* (?Tadcaster), before founding the house of *Streoneshalh*, Whitby. As abbess of Whitby she organised the regular life of the cloister, and succeeded in building up the monastery's reputation as a centre of learning to such a height that, as Bede reports, five bishops were chosen from among the inmates. 'So great was her wisdom that not only ordinary people, but kings and leaders, too, in their difficulties sought counsel from her, and found it.'

Anglo-Saxon women were sometimes considerable land-owners in their own right. Some place-names suggest this, as Adderbury, Oxfordshire, 'Eadburg's manor'; Wolverhampton, 'Wulfrun's chief estate'; Wissington, Suffolk, 'Wigswith's farmstead'; Abram, Lancashire, 'Eadburg's farm'. The eleventh-century will of Leofgifu disposed of a dozen estates in Suffolk and Essex, while Wynflaed left land in Wiltshire, Berkshire, Hampshire, Oxfordshire and Somerset. An estate at Ebbesborne, Wiltshire, she left to her daughter Aethelflaed with the specific instruction that it should be 'a perpetual inheritance to dispose of as she pleases'. A surviving record of a court case illustrates the freedom a woman could use in dealing with her estate. At a shire meeting at Aylton, Herefordshire, in the early eleventh century one Edwin, Enniaun's son, brought a claim against his mother for possession of a piece of land. The meeting sent three thanes to examine the woman's case, 'and she became very angry with her son, and summoned her kinswoman Leofflaed, Thorkil's wife, and said to her in their presence, "Here sits my kinswoman Leofflaed to whom I grant after my death my land, my gold, my clothing and apparel, and every-thing I own." And then she said to the thanes, "Act like thanes, and announce truthfully my message in the presence of all the worthy men at the meeting. Tell them to whom I have granted my land and all my possessions, leaving nothing at all to my own son. Ask them to be witnesses of this."' The thanes made their report, and Thorkil claimed the land, asking the meeting to reject Edwin's counter-claim, which they did. Whereupon Thorkil had the transaction entered for security on a blank page of a gospel-book in Hereford cathedral, where it still remains. The oral will, made before witnesses, gives a valid right to property. The eleventh-century will of Ketel shows women making formal agreements about the future of their property. Ketel arranged with his two sisters, Bote and Gode, for the inheritance of certain lands in East Anglia. Bote should have his estate at Ketteringham if he died first, but if she predeceased him, he should take her land at Somerleyton. A similar provision affected Ketel's property at Walsingham and Gode's at Preston.

A woman who owned estates and the slaves who helped maintain them was clearly likely to be something more than a lay figure, subordinate to her husband. In any case, many freewomen would be responsible for running households of some size, and this would involve directing servants, preparing stocks of food and supervising the work of the home, which would include baking, brewing, preserving, spinning and weaving. As the laws of Cnut remind us, the woman kept the store-room. Cnut asserts that a man may bring anything he wishes into his own house, but if it is stolen property his wife could not be held as an accessory unless it is found under her lock and key. She is to look after the keys of her store-room, chest and coffer, and is liable to prosecution if stolen property is discovered inside any of them. In women's graves north of the Thames there have often been found pairs of bronze, key-shaped 'girdle-hangers', which were worn hanging from the belt. They seem to have no practical function, and may have symbolised the woman's responsibility for her store-chest.

Key-like girdle-hangers from Little Wilbraham, Cambridgeshire

Care for a woman's financial security was largely in her family's hands. Perhaps significant of this is the fact that a woman kept her father's *wergild* status, rather than taking her husband's. Many of the appropriate provisions were customary, but some are preserved in the laws. Those of Aethelberht of Kent record that a wife who bears a living child is entitled to half her husband's goods if he dies. If the marriage was childless the woman's kinsmen can claim her own personal property and her *morgengyfu*, 'morning-gift', the present made her by her husband the morning after the marriage was consummated. Ine's laws do something to protect the innocent wife of a criminal. If her husband steals cattle and takes them to his farm, the wife is innocent 'if she dares to declare on oath that she did not taste the stolen meat'. Then, if the thief's possessions are confiscated, she has a right to keep one-third. A late text defines the ordering of the betrothal of a woman. Most of the provisions are financial, and it is only at the end that the writer points out that there should be a priest at the marriage, and that the man and woman concerned should not be related within the prohibited degrees. The consent of both the woman herself and her kinsmen is needed. The man must pledge to maintain the woman properly, must announce what he will give her for accepting his suit, and what she will get if he predeceases her—this, says the writer, should be half his goods, or all if they have a child together, unless she remarries. The man is to give securities for carrying out his promises, and the kinsmen must continue to look after the woman's interests. A couple of eleventh-century marriage agreements confirm this general statement. When Wulfric wished to marry archbishop Wulfstan's sister, the negotiated terms required that Wulfric 'promised her the land at Orleton and Ribbesford for her lifetime, and the land at Knightwick . . . and he gave her the land at Alton to give and to grant to whomsoever she pleased during her lifetime or after her death; and he promised her 50 mancuses of gold and 30 men and 30 horses.' These promises were witnessed by officials, members of the kin 'and many good men besides, both clerical and lay'. A Kentish contract stipulated the payment of a pound of gold to the woman for accepting the suit, and grants of land, together with 30 oxen, 20 cows, 10 horses and 10 slaves. Duplicate copies were made of both agreements, and deposited for security at religious houses.

Besides land, men and stock, a woman might own considerable personal property. Wynflaed's will lists jewellery, cups of silver and other material, chests and furniture, bedclothing and other hangings and seat covers, clothes and cloth, two buffalo (or aurochs) horns, a number of horses, broken and unbroken, as well as 'books and little things like that'. Possessions like these needed protection, and, where the kin could not give it, a woman

73

could appeal to her lord or the king. A grant made by Aethelred the Unready in 996 shows the turbulence of his reign and the measures he took to keep order. The grant concerns land forfeited by a criminal called Wulfbald, and properly defines his crimes. The first is that, 'when his father was dead, he went to his stepmother's land, and seized everything he found, inside and out, great and small'. Wulfbald ignored all the king's orders to make restitution, and died still in possession of the property. His widow and son continued the aggression, and Aethelred ultimately brought a successful suit against them, took the land in dispute and gave it to his mother. In a slightly later case Aethelred was more effective. When ealdorman Aelfric seized lands belonging to a widow called Eadflaed, he was exiled from the country. At the plea of some of his leading men Aethelred returned the property to the widow, who, at her death, left it in gratitude to the king.

So far, I have spoken of women only of the upper, or at least the freeborn class. Of poorer women and of the slaves we hear very little. Some of the more popular literature gives us brief glances of them at work. An indelicate riddle describes a churl's wife picking onions from their bed, peeling and cooking them. Another deals with yeast-baking with a wealth of double meanings. In a third a slavewoman, dark-complexioned and Celtic, threshes, while in a fourth a similar figure, this time drunken and half-witted, works with leather. The jay or magpie is compared to a *scirenige*, 'actress, female jester'. Among the female slaves bequeathed by Wynflaed were a weaver and a sempstress. The old nurse in the family of Leoba, abbess of Tauberbischofsheim, was a slave, rewarded with liberty for her prophecy of Leoba's coming glory. The laws of Aethelberht of Kent mention the king's grinding-slave, and the nobleman or churl's cup-bearer or serving maid. The *Rectitudines* describes the cheese-maker's office and her entitlement to 100 cheeses and most of the buttermilk. The same text defines the female slave's provisioning, which is less than that for a man: 'For a female slave eight pounds of corn for food, one sheep or threepence for winter food, one sester of beans for lenten food, whey in summer or one penny.'

Grave finds do something to fill out this meagre picture of woman's everyday life, though inevitably they record that of the richer classes of society. Grave-goods include cylindrical work-boxes of bronze, sometimes containing shreds of wool fibre or thread, bronze needles, iron shears, bone or stone spindle whorls, quern stones, cooking pots and bone or iron weaving swords, the latter apparently a symbol of wealth since they occur only in a few richly furnished burials. More sinister is the rare occurrence of a female skeleton thrown unceremoniously into a pagan grave on top of a carefully placed male body. Scandinavian parallels suggest that this is human sacrifice, the burial of a slave or companion for the dead man. Slightly different but equally sinister is a find at Sewerby, Yorkshire, where archaeologists came upon a rich woman's grave of the mid sixth to mid seventh centuries. Her kin had buried her carefully, in a coffin in a deep grave. They threw in a few inches

Goods found in a rich woman's grave include a thread box, spindle whorls, shears, girdle-hangers, a strike-a-light, and a cowrie shell amulet

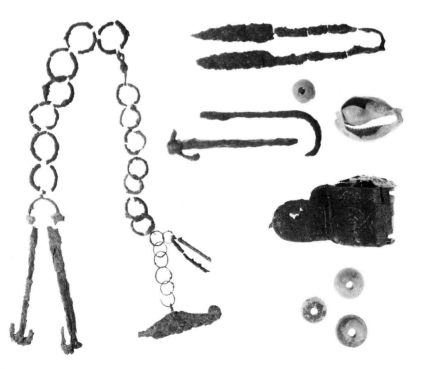

Part of St Cuthbert's maniple

of earth, and then a woman, whose body, lying face downwards, was contorted as though she had died violently. Across her pelvis rested part of a quern stone, hurled in to keep her down before the grave was closed. Was this, too, a slave sacrificed so that she could serve her mistress in death as in life?

Of the work done by Anglo-Saxon women little of artistic importance survives. Noteworthy are two pieces of embroidery. The most famous is the Bayeux tapestry. More sophisticated is the small group of materials from St Cuthbert's tomb, now preserved in Durham cathedral. A stole and two maniples bear texts showing that they were originally commissioned by queen Aelfflaed for bishop Frithestan of Winchester in the early tenth century. The delicacy and skill of workmanship suggest a long-standing practice of fine embroidery. There are enough references to show that this was commonly in women's hands. For instance, an early ninth-century charter of bishop Denewulf of Worcester grants lands in Hereford to one Eanswith on condition that she 'renews, cleans and extends the hangings of the church', and the earliest life of St Dunstan tells how a noble-woman called Aethelwynn invited the saint to design a stole for her to embroider and adorn with gold and precious stones. The *Liber Eliensis* records the case of a lady Aethelswith, who lived at Coveney, Cambridgeshire, spurning male society, preferring to spend her time with her maidens at orphrey work, tapestry-

Woman's dress

making and sewing vestments for the church. Clearly, Anglo-Saxon women often took to heart the proverb, 'A woman's place is at her embroidery.' Indeed, the nuns of Coldingham came to grief through their devotion to fine textile design. The Irishman Adamnan had a vision in which a heavenly messenger complained of the nuns' worldliness, in that they 'abandon the propriety of their calling, spending their time weaving fine clothes . . . either to adorn themselves like brides or to attract the attention of strangers'. The nuns ignored his warning, and the convent was very properly destroyed by God's fire.

Further Reading

A good if prosaic translation of *Beowulf* for use in connection with the material of this chapter is that of E. Talbot Donaldson. A large selection of poetry is translated in R. K. Gordon, *Anglo-Saxon Poetry*. The Old English wills are edited and translated in Dorothy Whitelock, *Anglo-Saxon Wills*. For Aethelflaed's career, see F. T. Wainwright, 'Æthelflæd Lady of the Mercians', in P. Clemoes, *The Anglo-Saxons*. The treasures related to St Cuthbert, including the stole and maniples, are described in C. F. Battiscombe, *The Relics of Saint Cuthbert*.

VI

The Working Man

In the late tenth or early eleventh century, Aelfric, master of the oblates at Cerne Abbas, Dorset, and subsequently abbot of Eynsham, near Oxford, compiled a short Latin text whose purpose was to give beginners practice in speaking Latin. The *Colloquy*, as it is called, is in dialogue form, bringing in a good deal of day-to-day Latin vocabulary, and often using the word-lists prepared for students' use. To give interest to his material, Aelfric cast it as a set of questions and answers, the master enquiring as though of people in different walks of life, the pupils framing appropriate replies. Thus, purely as a by-product of the educational process, Aelfric preserved a picture of the working life of Anglo-Saxon England. His characters are of the *ceorl* or slave classes: ploughman, shepherd, oxherd, huntsman, fisherman, fowler, merchant, cobbler, salter, baker, cook, smith, carpenter. Each discusses his trade. The ploughman, a slave, is hard-worked, toiling in wretched conditions through the bitter winter. He is up at daybreak, drives oxen to the field, yokes them, fits share and coulter to the plough, and must complete at least an acre of land a day, helped only by the lad who goads the beasts. He fodders his oxen, waters them and mucks out the

Ploughing and sowing

Ships

shippon. The shepherd brings his flock from fold to pasture and back, and with his dogs guards it against wolves. From time to time he moves the pens, and he milks the ewes twice a day, and makes cheese and butter. The oxherd leads the unyoked oxen to pasture after their day's work, watches them through the night, returning them next day fed and watered. The king's huntsman, the fisherman and the fowler describe their different techniques of working. Some beasts the huntsman drives into nets, and then stabs; the swift-footed he runs down with hounds; the boar he ambushes and spears, though it is dangerous. He gives his quarry to the king, who in return feeds and clothes him, and rewards him with gifts of horses and rings. The fisherman works in the rivers and estuaries, though he admits his more daring colleagues venture out on to the open sea, some even going in search of whales. He uses nets, hooks and bait, or creels, catching trout, lampreys, eels and pike. He sells his catch in the towns, and boasts that the demand is in excess of supply. The fowler commands several methods, trapping with nets, snares or bird-lime, decoying by whistles, using trained hawks. The hawks he takes as fledglings in the autumn, tames them and flies them over the winter. In spring he sets them free so as to avoid keeping them through the summer. He thinks it cheaper to train new birds each year, though some of his fellows disagree. The merchant rows across the seas, returning with silk and other rare cloths, with gems, gold, spices or perfumes, wine, oil, ivory, brass, bronze and tin, sulphur and glass. The cobbler cures skins and makes a variety of objects: slippers, shoes, gaiters, leather bottles, reins, halters, straps and purses. The salter boasts of his trade, for without it the cellars and storehouses would be empty. Salt is needed for preserving, for making butter and cheese, and for seasoning greens. Baker, cook, carpenter and different sorts of smith are briefly mentioned and the conversation ends with a dispute as to which trade is the most important. The speakers conclude that all are interdependent. All rely on the producers of food, but they in

79

turn must have the blacksmith to provide ploughshares, coulters and goads, fish-hooks, and awls, borers and needles, and the carpenter for houses, ships, bowls and buckets.

Other material confirms the details of Aelfric's account. The danger of cattle-rustling, which made the oxherd's job necessary, is shown by the elaborate provisions made in some legal codes for the trailing, tracing and identifying of stolen beasts, while there is on record the regrettable case of the delinquent Helmstan, formerly owner of land at Fonthill, Wiltshire, who first got into trouble for purloining a belt, but was finally ruined because 'he stole the untended oxen at Fonthill . . . and there was discovered, and the man who tracked him recovered the traced cattle. And Helmstan ran off, but a bramble scratched his face, and when he wanted to deny the accusation, this was brought in evidence against him.' To prevent trading in stolen cattle Edgar's code required that a man buying live-stock must 'announce it when he comes home' and 'bring it on to the common pasture with the witness of his village' on pain of forfeiture of the beasts. Hunters and fowlers are commonly referred to. Charters often list the appurtenances of an estate, including 'fowling-grounds and hunting-grounds', and some grant freedom from such services to the king as 'entertainment of . . . keepers of dogs, or horses, or hawks.' Brihtric and Aelfswith bequeathed to their royal lord 'two hawks and all his staghounds', while prince Athelstan left to his staghuntsman 'the stud which is on Coldridge'. In *Beowulf*, Hrothgar describes the dreadful mere in which the monster Grendel and his mother lived: 'Though the heath-stepper, the hart strong in its antlers, hard-pressed by the hounds, seeks the forest after a long chase, he will rather give up his life on the bank than plunge into the mere and hide his head there.' Aelfric's huntsman went after harts, boars, roedeer, goats and hares. To these the Exeter Riddle 15 seems to add the badger. *The Fates of Men* gives further details of the fowler in his capacity as falconer: 'Another shall tame the proud wild bird, the hawk on the hand . . . put jesses on it, and so feed the proud-feathered bird in its fetters, weaken the swift flyer with small morsels of food, until the Welsh falcon becomes humble to its feeder, trained to the young

Fowling

man's hand', and there are numerous general references to hawking in the poetry, as the Cottonian gnomic verse's 'the hawk, though wild, shall abide on the glove'. Fisheries too are often listed in the charters. From Edward the Confessor's reign survives a survey of an estate at Tidenham, Gloucestershire, situated where the Wye and Severn meet. It lists 101 basket weirs and four hackle weirs, contrivances for catching fish in these difficult tidal waters. Every second fish caught at the weirs is the perquisite of the lord of the manor, as is every rare fish of value—sturgeon, porpoise and sea fish are specifically named. A roughly contemporary lease of the same land provides for the annual payment of six porpoises and 30,000 herrings. Property given to the fenland abbey of Thorney included money for ships and nets at Farcet and Whittlesey Mere, both in Huntingdonshire, and the rent charged on some of the fen is measured in thousands of eels and in 'sticks', that is quantities of fish strung on a skewer. When Wulfric Spott bequeathed to his kinsmen Aelfhelm and Wulfheah lands between the Ribble and the Mersey and in the Wirral, he stipulated that each should pay the monastery at Burton 3,000 shad during the fishing season. An estate at Conisbrough on the Don went to Aelfhelm on condition that the monks received a third of the annual catch of fish. Place-names record settlements of hunters, fishermen and fowlers: Huntingford in Dorset and Gloucestershire, Hunton in Kent, Fisherton in Wiltshire and Fiskerton, with its Old Norse variant of the word 'fisher', near the Trent in Nottinghamshire, and Fullerton in Hampshire.

From the charters it is clear that salt-making was an important industry. In the early eighth century king Aethelbald of Mercia exchanged some land with the community at Worcester, giving them 'a certain portion of ground on which salt is customarily made, at the south side of the river called Salwarp . . . for the construction of three salthouses and six furnaces, receiving in exchange . . . six other furnaces in two salthouses in which also salt is made, on the north side of the said river'. Some years later Aethelberht II of Kent granted to the priest and abbot Dunn 'a quarter of one ploughland by the river Lympne suitable for the boiling of salt', and with it an annual gift of 120 wagons of wood for the heating. The appurtenances of the monastery of Hanbury, Worcestershire, listed in the ninth century, include 'salt-pits and lead-furnaces'. Such place-names as Saltings and Budleigh Salterton, Devon, and Seasalter, Kent, contain the word *saltærn*, 'building where salt was made or sold'; Salt, Staffordshire, seems to mean 'salt-pit', and there are still saltworks in the neighbourhood; and the element *saltere*, 'maker or seller of salt', occurs in names like Salterford, Nottinghamshire, Salter's bridge, Staffordshire, Sawtry, Huntingdonshire, often indicating the roads or river-crossings which served the distribution of salt.

Though the smith 'in his smithy gives us nothing but iron firesparks and the clangour of beating sledge-hammers and blowing bellows', even Aelfric recognised that he was one of the most important of workmen, providing many of the tools and utensils, as well as the weapons, coins and jewellery of Anglo-Saxon England. The word 'smithy' occurs in a number of place-names, like Smeeth, Kent, and Smitha, Devon, and the word 'smith' is in Smeaton, Yorkshire, and Smethwick, Staffordshire. His trade is one of those listed in *The Endowments of Men*, which shows him 'forging many a weapon for use in warfare, when, for men's strife, he makes helmet or dagger or mail-coat, bright sword or shield's boss, firmly

The smith

82

The Sittingbourne, Kent, scramasax, with its maker's name, Biorhtelm, inlaid in the blade

fixed against the spear's thrust'. The laws of Ine provide that if a man of the *gesith* class moves his dwelling he may take with him his three important servants, reeve, smith and children's nurse, and Alfred's laws have a provision which makes a smith or a sword-polisher responsible for crimes committed with weapons or tools in their charge. Presumably each settlement would have at least one man capable of blacksmith's work of one quality or another, and the great inventory of Anglo-Saxon metalwork, swords, spearheads, knives, scythe-blades, hammer-heads, adzes, axeheads, spade-shoes, fish-hooks, picks, borers, needles, strap-ends, buckles, brooches, pendants, coins, keys, locks, bowls, buckets, cups, censer-covers, rings, spoons, shield-bosses, seal-dies, and so on, shows something of the range of skill of the Anglo-Saxon smith. His material came from the smelting-shops of which many traces survive from Anglo-Saxon times— iron-slag heaps at Witton and Thetford, Norfolk, and Botesdale, Suffolk, and hearths also at Grimstone End, Pakenham, Suffolk, for example. The occupation-name *orablawere*, 'ore-blower, smelter', occurs in the place-name Kirkby Overblow, Yorkshire, while such place-names as Orgreave, Yorkshire, Orgrave, Lancashire, and Orsett, Essex, have the element *ora*, 'ore', either in allusion to metal-workings or to the digging of bog-ore. A site at West Runton, Norfolk, was fairly intensively exploited between 850 and 1150. The workers dug iron-stone pebbles from pits cut in the sand, and smelted them in furnaces built on the site. The yield was small for the effort expended; it is calculated that some 270 cubic feet of sand had to be dug away to give 600 lb of iron-bearing pebbles, and these

Digging. The wooden spade has an iron shoe

83

The shepherd

might produce 150 lb of iron.

I have spoken already of the position and importance of the merchant. Of the other occupations which Aelfric portrays we hear comparatively little in the written sources, though archaeology supplies illustrative material in many cases. As a young man St Cuthbert was a shepherd. With a number of companions he seems to have taken up to the hill pastures flocks of sheep drawn from several different farms. It was while on night-watch on one of these expeditions that he saw the vision of St Aidan's soul entering the heavenly kingdom which led him to the monastic life. Scattered about the north country were shepherd's bothies, occupied only during the summer, and this suggests that, as in modern Scandinavia, parts of Anglo-Saxon England had a *saeter* economy. Of the tanner's work we read in Exeter Riddle 12. Describing the ox, it says, 'If life is taken from me, I bind firmly the dark Welsh. . . . Sometimes I give a brave man drink from my bosom'; the prepared skin is made into ropes and leather bottles. Further light on this trade comes from Hungate, York, whose water-logged site preserved several late Anglo-Saxon shoes. Apparently a cobbler threw them out as being past repair, for they have pieces cut from them to patch newer shoes and they were found in company with strips and snippets of hide, the refuse of a leatherworker's shop, and a bone-handled short knife, which may have been one of his tools. The soles of the shoes are of cattle-hide, the uppers are single pieces of deerskin. Both are prepared with vegetable tannins, and the two are sewn together with leather thongs. *The Endowments of Men* pictures the carpenter-joiner who can 'firmly frame the great hall against sudden collapse', but there is surprisingly little mention elsewhere of the woodworker who supplied a great proportion of the material goods of Anglo-

84

Saxon England, from houses and ships down to bowls, buckets and cups. Fortunately, numbers of his tools survive. His most versatile implement—though it could also be a weapon—was the axe, used for felling, trimming and cutting up his timber, and probably also for initial smoothing, and, in view of the state of some axe butts, as a hammer. Wedges were employed for splitting timber, adzes for shaping it, and gouges and boring-bits for hollowing out. Two Anglo-Saxon saw-blades are known. For smoothing the wood there was the drawknife, of which a single specimen survives, from Sandtun, Kent. From Sarre, in the same county, is a small cabinet-maker's plane, with a stock of antler and a bronze base-plate. Some carpenters must have had more elaborate equipment such as lathes, for there is the occasional turned object, like the maple-wood bowl found at Hungate, York.

There were, of course, many trades not represented in the *Colloquy*. Preserved in place-names are occupational terms like *colere* or *colestre*, 'charcoal-burner' (Colsterworth, Lincolnshire); *pottere*, 'potter' (Potterne, Wiltshire); *sapere*, 'soap-maker' or 'soap-dealer' (Sapperton, Derbyshire); *walcere*, 'fuller' (Walkern, Hertfordshire); *webba*, 'weaver' (Webland, Devon). Archaeological finds are often revealing in this context. At Old Erringham, Sussex, was traced the site of a weaving-hut, 16 by 11 feet, cut into the chalk. There were 75 loom-weights in two groups, evidence of two large looms. At Upton, Northamptonshire, were 36 loom-weights in a sunken-floored hut. At Grimstone End clay loom weights lay in two lines, 8 feet long and

Boat-building

Builders and carpenters

8–9 inches apart, 30 in the one and 32 in the other. This could represent dramatically a collapsed or burnt loom, but the excavators think it more likely that they were laid out thus for firing, to be covered with heaped brushwood sealed with turf. At West Stow, Suffolk, an early weaving-village has been identified on a site of some two acres of knoll, surrounded in Anglo-Saxon times by marsh or water. Excavation (1966) uncovered 14 huts, six of them for domestic use. Loom-weight finds show that three others were weaving-sheds, and yet another, which contained fragmentary double-edged combs that had undergone hard wear, was probably a carding-shed. Three huts with sparse finds may have served to store wool or cloth. From Winchester there is evidence of bell-founding, in a late tenth-century pit with fragments of clay-moulds. Several Anglo-Saxon sites have pottery kilns. At Ipswich, for instance, five kilns have been examined, one of the middle period (seventh to ninth century) and four from the later. The two most complete examples were circular and oval respectively, roughly four feet in diameter, with clay linings. Cassington, Oxfordshire, has revealed 20 hut sites in two groups, perhaps discrete communities not necessarily contemporary. Several crafts are represented: weaving, iron-working, bronze-casting and pottery-making. There are two pottery kilns, dug into the gravel. Each has a stoke-pit linked to a smaller firing chamber, two or three feet across, and their walls were lined with lime-covered wattle.

Eddius's *Life of St Wilfrid* describes the repair of York Minster by craftsmen who renewed the roof ridges, leaded the roof and glazed the windows. The Anglo-Saxons must have had numbers of competent masons, such as built Wilfrid's churches at Ripon and Hexham, or worked at Breamore, Hampshire, Brixworth, Northamptonshire, or on Edward the Confessor's Westminster. Large-scale building operations like these would require industrial organisation, and hosts of workers in subsidiary occupations, providing the wood scaffolding and timber shoring, the thatch or shingle for the roofs, and the stucco work, glazed wall-tiles or window-glass which was sometimes used. There must also have been skilled quarrymen in such areas as Barnack, Bath and Portland. Recent occasional finds of poorly made bricks, as in the castle mound at Oxford, suggest another Anglo-Saxon industry.

The Anglo-Saxon nave and tower of Brixworth church

The *Life of St Wilfrid* mentions the jewellers the saint employed to make an elaborate gold case for a gospel-book he had written, and the *Lindisfarne Gospels* seems once to have had a similar cover. Exeter Riddle 26 describes the making of a book: cleaning, drying and preparing the vellum, writing the text, encasing it in leather, and adding jewelled decoration and metal clasps.

Athelstan's second law-code contains provisions for securing the honesty

of moneyers, who in this context seem to be the craftsmen who actually make the royal coinage, and of shield-
makers, who are forbidden to use sheepskin for their
wares.

Clearly there is plenty of evidence for Anglo-Saxon industrial
activity. Yet Aelfric was right in putting the main stress in his
Colloquy on the producers of food, on the ploughman 'because the
ploughman feeds us all', and to a less extent on the fisherman,
fowler and oxherd. In a society of primitive technology like that
of the Anglo-Saxons the vast majority of people must have been
food-producers, and it is the more unfortunate that we have
little knowledge of their daily life and methods and conditions
of work. Clearly, too, daily life would vary enormously over the
different parts of the country and the different centuries of our
period: according to the nature of the land and its state of
clearance or drainage; according to whether a community were
newly set up or long established; according as times and climates
were favourable or unhelpful; according as the local economic
situation rendered large-scale development or investment
possible or not. The Anglo-Saxons did not come to a virgin land,
and some of their early fields were probably superimposed upon
Romano-British ones. But most early settlements would involve
a lot of clearing of scrub and forest by burning (compare the element *bryne*, 'place cleared by burning' in Brilley, Herefordshire,
for example) or rooting up the stumps of trees (compare the
place-name element *styfecing* from the verb *styfician*, 'root up').
Cleared land would be ploughed, and turned gradually into us-
able arable land—in Exeter Riddle 21 the ox, pulling the plough,
is called 'the grey enemy of the forest', and in Riddle 38 he is
described as breaking the hill-country. An agricultural community could thus consist of a group of people capable of breaking in land in this way, and then keeping it efficiently under
cultivation, the food supply supplemented by the quarry from
hunting, fowling and fishing, and by the beasts that could be
pastured on the nearby heath, waste or wood. Pasture was very
important in the early stages of settlement, and remained
economically significant throughout. Legal documents disposing
of estates commonly list the pastures linked to them. For

Pasturing pigs

example, in 822 Ceolwulf I of Mercia granted to archbishop Wulfred land in Kent bordering upon Andred, that is, upon the great forest which occupied the Weald. The grant included 'in Andred, food and pasture for swine and cattle or goats in its places Ewehurst, *Sciofingden* and *Snadhyrst*'. Aelfhelm bequeathed an estate at Brickenden, Hertfordshire, to St Peter's, Westminster, but reserved certain pasture rights, requiring that 'when there is mast, 200 pigs be fed for my wife's sake, to benefit whatever foundation she pleases'. Exeter Riddle 40 speaks of 'the mast-filled pig, the grunting black boar, which has had a happy life in the beech-wood', while *The Runic Poem* defines *ac*, 'oak-tree', as 'bacon-fodder'.

On these pastures grazed cattle, sheep, goats, pigs and horses. It is usually said that the pig was the most common of the beasts: certainly he features prominently in the written sources. What little close examination there has been of animal bones from settlement sites suggests there was a good deal of local variation in pastoral practice. The bones at Maxey, Northamptonshire, show the following ratios: cattle 36 per cent: sheep or goats 36 per cent: pigs 11 per cent: the rest, horses, dogs, cats, domestic fowl and other birds. Worked out in poundages this shows that by far the greatest element—58 per cent—of the meat diet was beef, with about 11 per cent of mutton and goat, and only five per cent of pork. At Cassington, Oxfordshire, however, 43 per cent of the bones found were cattle, 29 per cent pig and only 12 per cent sheep, while at Crossgates, Yorkshire, the ox accounted for about 60 per cent of the bones discovered, the horse 30 per cent and the pig 10 per cent. Again, it is usually claimed that most beasts were slaughtered at the beginning of winter, a few

Slaughtering

only being left alive to breed from next spring. The Maxey findings do not confirm this. About 54 per cent of its cattle lived at least one winter, about 35 per cent at least two, while over 20 per cent were at least three years old. On the other hand, over a third of the pigs were killed at less than a year old, and two-thirds at less than 18 months. An interesting fact is that none of the Maxey horses reached ripe age, and the excavators suggest that this animal worked as a draught or riding beast until about five, and was then slaughtered for food.

In describing the exploitation of arable land, we are hampered by inadequate evidence. Many of our conclusions remain speculative. This is a field where archaeology has as yet made little impact, and practically no Anglo-Saxon ploughing equipment has survived: ploughshares from Thetford and St Neots, and perhaps a coulter from Westley Waterless, though the identification is uncertain. Scholars have warned us against taking Anglo-Saxon drawings of the implement too seriously, for artists probably copied from other drawings, which may have been of non-English inspiration, instead of from actual ploughs of their own countryside. The only close description of ploughing is Exeter Riddle 21 (which is also a typical example of the Anglo-Saxon riddle form): 'My nose points downwards. I crawl along, digging into the ground. I go as the grey enemy of the forest guides me, and my lord, my guard, who walks stooping at my tail. He twists me on the plain, lifts me and presses me on, and sows in my track. I nose my way forwards, brought from the wood, skilfully constructed, carried on a wain. I have many strange properties. As I walk, there is green on one side of me, on the other my dark track is clear. Driven through my back, hanging beneath me, is a well-sharpened point. Another in my head, firm and forward-facing, leans to the side, so that I tear

90

with my teeth if I am well served from behind by the man who is my lord.'

Thus we know that the Anglo-Saxon plough had a coulter to cut the field vertically, and a share to cut the bottom of the furrow, but we do not know how heavy it was, whether it was wheeled or whether it had a mouldboard to turn the furrow. We do not know how many oxen—the standard draught animal rather than the slighter horse—were needed to pull it. It is usually assumed that the plough was of a heavy type, requiring a team of eight beasts. This would be more than the average *ceorl* possessed, and so developed the practice of co-aration, whereby a number of *ceorls* banded together to supply the equipment, and together ploughed the arable land, which was arranged in a number of large open fields cleared from the waste. They would plough each field in strips, long and narrow because that was the most convenient shape for a heavy four-, six- or eight-ox plough, and these would be allotted to the various partners in the enterprise in turn. Thus each man had a chance to sow a strip as soon as it became available, as well as of getting a due share of good and bad land equally with his mates. Crops sown, as far as the sparse evidence goes, were wheat, oats, rye and barley (with perhaps a preference for the hardy and free-yielding barley which would give malt for brewing as well as cereal food), and probably beans, peas and lentils as well. Presumably in most areas the open fields were divided into pairs, so that in any one year one could be sowed, the other left fallow to keep the land in good heart. The fallow, too, must be ploughed at a convenient time, and was grazed or mown for fodder, as suggested by the place-name elements *filethe*, 'hay got from the fallow land' (as in Fawley, Hampshire) and *mæd*, 'mowing grass, meadow'. Communal duties in the

Mowing

fields did not end with the ploughing, for reaping may have been done cooperatively. Moreover, each *ceorl* had the personal responsibility for fencing-in his own sections, as a law of Ine records: 'If *ceorls* have a common meadow or other land divided in shares to fence, and some have fenced their portion and some have not, and if cattle eat up their common crops or grass, those who are responsible for the gap are to go and pay to the others who have fenced their part compensation for the damage done there.'

This, then, is the traditional picture of the sturdy, independent, Anglo-Saxon peasant, owning his acre-strips in the open fields, and living in his cottage, which had its own garth where he could grow vegetables and such fruit as apples and pears (compare such place-names as Appleton and Perreton). His beasts he kept on the common pasture, where he had rights, and he relied on the uncleared forests for fuel, timber for buildings and wagons, hurdle-poles and tools. He was more or less self-supporting, and could keep himself above subsistence level in good years, though he must take certain supplies (salt, metals, luxury wares) from pedlars and merchants, paying for them with his surplus. He held an important voice in the village councils, and was protected in law by his position as a freeman.

This is, of course, a drastic oversimplification, for on the face of it it cannot be true for the whole of Anglo-Saxon England in time and place. Conditions of tenure were different in different parts of the country. The open-field system, though very common, was not universal. Agriculture must have varied according to local conditions: for instance, the chain of place-names with the element *wic*, 'dairy-farm', along the marshlands of the Essex coast suggests that the district flourished on sheep pasture rather than arable farming, and this might demand a different type of social organisation. The picture I have drawn so far leaves no place for a man's lord, nor is there any suggestion that a *ceorl's* freedom might be limited by obligatory services which he owed in return for his land. There is no mention of leasing of land, which we know took place.

As early as the laws of Ine (preserved, however, only in a recension from Alfred's reign) we find the notable provision: 'If anyone covenants for a yardland or more at a fixed rent, and ploughs it, if the lord wishes to increase for him the rent of the land by demanding service as well as rent, he need not accept it if the lord does not give him a dwelling; but then he must forfeit the crops', which seems clear evidence, even at this date, that occupation of land might involve services and rent paid by a freeman to a social superior. The agricultural history of Anglo-Saxon England shows a gradual decline in the *ceorl*'s position, and a rise in that of the lord who could organise large-scale economic development. I quote two cogent pieces of evidence, one archaeological, one manuscript, for such large-scale exploitation. The mill was an important piece of equipment in the later period, notably in the east of the country. Over 5,600 are recorded in Domesday Book. Most of these would be water-mills, though occasional references to mill-oxen show that some used animal-power. At Old Windsor, Berkshire, Dr Hope-Taylor's excavations revealed traces of a very large mill. Associated buildings seem to have been sumptuous, with tiled roof and glazed windows. The mill had three vertical wheels, running in parallel, served from a canal over 20 feet wide, dug for about three-quarters of a mile across a loop of the Thames. At the time the mill was built—at the beginning of the ninth century—local woodlands were cleared. The whole looks like a major agricultural development—involving considerable capital investment—which aimed at preparing land for grain crops and supplying the mills to process them.

From the eleventh century is a short tract called *Be gescead-wisan gerefan*, 'On the competent reeve', describing the duties of the steward of an estate, and the abilities he must have. It includes a list of tools needed for a big farm: axe, adze, billhook, borer, plane, saw, clamping-iron, auger, mattock, ?crowbar, share, coulter, goad, scythe, sickle, hoe, spade, shovel, woad-dibble, flail, winnowing-fan, barrow, broom, mallet, rake, fork, ladder, curry-comb, shears, tongs, scales, wagon-covers, ploughing and harrowing tackle, a large range of implements for spinning and weaving, and for such specialised occupations as milling, leatherwork and plumbing, and a variety of household utensils like measures, cauldrons, ladles,

93

CANTICVM

Fencing

pans, pots, bowls, trivets, pitchers, tubs, churns, cheese-vats, baskets, sieves, containers for honey and salt, chests, coffers and so on. The steward must supervise the year's work, which is catalogued, beginning in early summer and carrying through to the following spring. In summer the labourers break up the fallow land, shear sheep, cut wood and weed, carry out dung, make hurdles and build and repair woodwork, make folds, fishing-weirs and mills. In autumn they reap and mow, dig up woad and gather in various crops, thatch and roof, clean out the folds, prepare the shippons and sties, and get the ploughing under way before winter. During winter the ploughing continues as long as the weather allows. When the frosts come, the men are largely occupied with the inside jobs, though they also prepare the garth for vegetables and fruit. They make stalls for the cattle, pens for the pigs, perches for the fowls, and kilns and ovens, and they cut wood and thresh. In spring there is more ploughing, beans are sown and young trees and vineyards set, ditches are dug and the hedges that keep out wild beasts are cut. As soon as the weather is fine, the men set madder, linseed and woad, and plant in the garths. Such an account may, of course, be misleading. It may list all the duties that could be required, not those which were needed in any one year. Yet the general impression is of a practical treatise on large-scale farming written by someone who knew what he was talking about. He concludes: 'I have spoken about what I know. Anyone who knows better may speak more.'

The *Rectitudines* deals with people who occupy an estate of this magnitude and complication of organisation. It begins by defining four ranks of men: thane, *geneat*, *cotsetla* (or 'cottar') and *gebur*. To the king the thane owes three great duties, armed service, repairing of fortresses and bridge-building, in respect of his land, but himself is lord of it. The *geneat* pays rent and a pig for pasturage each year, and may have services of a rather superior sort to perform for his lord: riding, carrying and grooming, reaping and mowing, cutting the 'deer-hedge', building and fencing, bringing strangers to the village, and

94

acting as his lord's guard. The cottar farms at least five acres of arable, and pays no rent. He must work on or with respect to his lord's demesne. In some areas he labours every Monday for his lord, or for three days a week during harvest. In some he reaps his lord's crops throughout August. Again, he may carry out obligations that lie upon the demesne, watching the coast or working at the king's 'deer-hedge'. The *gebur's* duties were often onerous. He must do his lord's tasks for two days a week throughout the year, and three in harvest and early spring. During the ploughing season he has to plough an acre of his lord's land a week, and provide seed for it, three acres in payment of rent, and two for pasturage. Another three acres he must plough and sow as 'tribute-land'. Rent was payable in money and in kind: tenpence at Michaelmas, 23 sesters of barley and two hens at Martinmas, one lamb or twopence at Easter. He gives six loaves to his lord's swineherd when the pigs are driven to pasture, and, with a fellow, supports one of his lord's hounds. When he enters upon his land, the *gebur* receives two oxen, one cow, six sheep and seven acres sown, with tools and utensils; when he dies, the lord takes what remains. Freeman he may have been, but the *gebur* was firmly under the lord's thumb.

The text goes on to describe the specialist workers: bee-keeper, swineherd, oxherd, cowherd, shepherd, goatherd, granary-keeper, beadle, woodward and hayward. Their customary services and dues are listed, as well as some of the perquisites appropriate to their offices: the shepherd gets 12 days' dung at Christmas, one lamb from the year's young ones, one bell-wether's fleece, the milk of his flock for a week after the equinox, and a bowl full of whey or buttermilk all summer,

Threshing and winnowing

Ploughing, hoeing and pruning

while the woodward has every tree blown down by the wind. Finally, there is a catalogue of general perquisites: winter provisions, Easter provisions, a harvest feast at reaping, a drinking-feast at ploughing, rewards for haymaking and rick-making, a log from each load at wood-carrying, 'and many things which I cannot recount'.

The writer is at pains to point out the variety of customs which apply throughout the country. Nevertheless, it is clear that by this time, in the eleventh century, the type of estate he is describing was common. In the Danelaw, as Domesday Book and other post-Conquest evidence shows, there still remained a numerous and powerful free peasantry, owing their lords some service, tribute and court attendance, but men of standing, owning their own lands and paying royal dues. From much of the rest of England the society of freemen, farming their own lands in the open fields and pasturing their beasts of right on the commons and wastes, had vanished—if indeed it had ever generally existed. In its place was a more closely knit type of agricultural organisation, a unit of larger scale with freemen of different social ranks, different offices and rights with respect to the land and their lord, and with specialist workers and slaves. Here customary law governed the relationship between men, land and lord. Each estate had its reeve or steward, one of whose responsibilities was to know the practice of the estate. 'This is why a man who does not wish to lose honour in the land must enjoy learning the customs used among the people.'

Further Reading

G. N. Garmonsway has edited *Aelfric's Colloquy*, without translation but with a useful introduction and notes. For the products of the smith in the later part of the period, see D. M. Wilson, *Catalogue of Ornamental Metalwork 700–1100*. A. H. Smith's *English Place-Name Elements*, English Place-Name Society, vols. xxv and xxvi, supplies much of the place-name material used here and elsewhere in the book. Bertram Colgrave edited and translated Eddius's *Life of Saint Wilfrid*, though the freer translation by J. F. Webb in *Lives of the Saints*, Penguin Classics, is more readily available. The Maxey finds are reported in *Medieval Archaeology*, vol. viii, 1964. C. S. and C. S. Orwin, *The Open Fields*, is the standard account of early agricultural organisation.

VII

King's Servants

There is no standard form of wording for an Anglo-Saxon royal
charter. A fairly typical example records king Edgar's sale of
land at Staunton, Herefordshire, to his thane Ealhstan. Much
of its text is in Latin. It begins in a flowery style, commenting
upon the swift passing of earthly things, and Christ's purchase
of eternal glory by the sacrifice of his worldly body; so it gets
on to the subject of buying and selling. This is why the charter
exists, to give permanence to a business agreement, preserving
its terms for present and future landholders. Then come the
terms of the transfer: 'Therefore I, Edgar, by the favour of
divine grace gaining the monarchy of the whole kingdom of the
Mercians, bestow and willingly concede to my faithful thane
Ealhstan for his acceptable money, namely 40 mancuses of
refined gold, a certain estate in the province of the *Magonsæte*,
that is, six hides in the place which is called by its inhabitants
Staunton, that he may have it and always possess it eternally,
with all benefits duly belonging to that land, and that he may
have the power to do with it whatever he wishes to do.' Then
follows the Old English schedule of boundaries, and the record
of a further grant of a house in Hereford. The conditions of sale
are: 'This land is to be free from all tribute, great and small,
and from royal service, except the construction of bridges, the
building of fortresses and military expedition.' Anyone who
tries to vary or diminish these terms is threatened with God's
wrath. Next comes the date, 958 in the second year of Edgar's
reign. Finally there is a list of witnesses to the business: the
king, six bishops, five ealdormen, six king's thanes, and a man
Byrhtnoth whose rank is not stated.

*Latin charter of Offa of Mercia granting land at Westbury on Trym to an officer
Aethelmund. Above are the terms of the grant, below the list of attesting witnesses*

A text deriving from Christ Church, Canterbury, exemplifies
a second, much simpler, formal document, the royal writ.
'King Cnut sends friendly greetings to bishop Eadsige and
abbot Aelfstan and Aethelric and all my thanes in Kent. And I

99

declare to you that I wish archbishop Aethelnoth to discharge his obligations on landed property belonging to the bishopric at the same rate now as he did before Aethelric was reeve, and after he was reeve to the present day. And I will not allow any wrong to be offered to the archbishop, whoever may be reeve.' The original manuscript carried the royal seal to guarantee its authenticity.

Writ and seal of Edward the Confessor recording the rights granted to archbishop Stigand and the community of Christ Church, Canterbury

These two documents illustrate how the king got things done, at any rate after his office had developed a strong formal authority with an organisation to give it effect. The charter witnesses are members of the king's council, which includes the

leaders of church and state. The people addressed in the writ
are members of the shire court of Kent, local religious and lay
authorities. The ealdormen, reeves and king's thanes mentioned are royal officials. The very existence of the writ implies
a royal writing office, however primitive, and the preservation
of the charter text, in the archives of Wells cathedral, shows how
evidence of land ownership was kept.

By his writ the king told his local representatives about
administrative decisions which they would have to put into
effect, or which they would need to know. The charter text
quoted shows how the king, in practical terms, made his
subjects work for him. He imposes three named duties on
Ealhstan in return for the land: army service, building fortresses and bridge-building. By explicitly excluding all other
royal dues, the charter implies that many holders of estates had
obligations beyond these three. Other charters, defining more
fully the freedoms they give, tell us what these obligations were.
Some give exemption from 'building the royal residence',
'pasturing the king's swine', or 'capturing a thief'. Others
relieve an estate from the entertainment of king and bishop
and of royal officials such as the ealdorman, reeve or tax-
gatherer. 'Neither shall there be sent there men who bear
hawks or falcons, or lead dogs or horses.' Charters may remove
the duty of feeding and putting up men whom 'we call in
Saxon *Walhfæreld* [the Welsh expedition]' or those 'we call in
Saxon *fæstingmen* [? the king's messengers]'. The monastery of
Blockley was not required to support 'mounted men of the
English race and foreigners, whether of noble or humble birth'
or 'huntsmen of the king or ealdormen except only those who
are in the province of the *Hwicce*'.

Phrases like these point to an elaborate royal household and
staff partly supported by dues and obligations laid upon many
landowners. In early times organisation was simpler, and the
king a man of meagre pomp with a small retinue of servants
and guards. He spent part of the year, as did the early kings of
Norway, progressing through his realm, entertained by each
of his nobles in turn. Thus perhaps was Aethelberht of Kent
in the early seventh century, for his laws prescribe special

compensation for crimes committed 'if the king is drinking at a man's house', and list *wergilds* for a few lower-class servants such as the royal *ambihtsmith*, 'serving-smith', messenger and grinding-slave.

In later times the king had his own broad lands on which he usually lived, moving from one to another to shift the burden of the court. Thus, Athelstan was at Colchester, Wellow, Wiltshire, and Lifton, Devon, in 931, at Milton Royal, Kent, and Amesbury, Wiltshire, in 932, and he spent Christmas 934 'at the royal manor at Frome'. The king's estates, each run by a reeve, contributed to his household's support, and a food-rent, *feorm* (whence our modern English word 'farm'), paid from such lands as had no charter exemption, also helped to maintain him. When Offa granted a total of 80 hides of land at Westbury on Trym and Henbury, Gloucestershire, to the church at Worcester, he released it 'from all compulsion of kings and ealdormen', but reserved from it 'these taxes: that is, of the tribute at Westbury, two tuns full of pure ale and a *cumb* [a measure of unknown size] full of mild ale and a *cumb* full of Welsh ale, and seven oxen and six wethers and 40 cheeses and six long *theru* [meaning unknown] and 30 "ambers" [another measure] of unground corn, and four "ambers" of meal.' These should be delivered at the royal manor most convenient to Westbury.

The laws and charters never define in detail the so-called *trimoda necessitas*, the three major duties imposed upon landowners. Scattered sources give us bits of information. Primary was military service. On this the laws tell us the penalties for desertion and for neglect of duty, but we do not know, in general at any rate, what proportion of the adult male population was liable to call-up and how they were chosen, for how long or how far afield they might serve, and what supplies and arms they need bring. In time of grave emergency the king could call out all able-bodied freemen. This was probably rare, though it happened in 1006 when Aethelred 'summoned out the whole nation from Wessex and Mercia, and they were on military service against the Danes the whole autumn'. More commonly we hear of the shire or district forces. At Rochester

These Anglo-Saxon soldiers fought at Hastings without defensive armour. They may be men of the fyrd, *distinguished thus from the royal bodyguard*

[national army]

in 999, for example, the Kentish *fyrd*, or militia, attacked a Viking army which put them to flight. In 1001 the men of Hampshire fought the Danes at Dean in Sussex, just beyond their county border. In 1003 a joint army from Hampshire and Wiltshire tried to intercept Swein's Vikings, but the English commanders were inept or treacherous, and the intruders marched unmolested to the sea. When well led the *fyrd* contained doughty fighters. In 1004 the Danes left Thetford, where they had encamped overnight, to get back to their fleet at Norwich. Ulfcytel, the East Anglian ealdorman, came up with his forces and a ferocious battle ensued in which 'the flower of the East Anglian people was killed. Had their full strength been there, the Danes would never have got back to their ships; for they themselves said that they had never met fiercer hand-play in England than Ulfcytel dealt them.' But the English were not always so well disciplined. Of the great army of 1006 the chronicler says wryly, 'the English levies [? perhaps the original means just 'the campaign'] caused the country people every sort of harm, so they got benefit from neither the native nor the invading army'.

Athelstan's law-code promulgated 'at Grately' required 'every man to have two mounted men for each plough', which presumably defines a landowner's military obligations, though it does not say who chose the two men or what social rank they held. Later, in Edward the Confessor's time, the common requirement was a lesser one of a man for every five hides of land, though individual estates had their own customary rules agreed upon with the king. Sometimes they commuted the service for a money payment, which the king used to hire mercenaries. Not all men qualified for the *fyrd* would be called up together, for the life of the countryside had to continue even under hostile attack. The *Chronicle* tells that Alfred 'divided his *fyrd* into two, so that there were always half of the men at home, half out on duty, except for the men whose job it was to defend the boroughs'. Thus he protected his realm with minimal loss to its economy.

The common arms of the Anglo-Saxon soldier were spear and shield. The spear, used for thrusting or throwing, had an iron head and ash shaft, and was about seven feet long. The shield was round, light and thin, its diameter varying between one and three feet. It was of limewood, sometimes of laminated construction, usually covered with leather and having a metal central boss which masked the hand-grip. Less common was the sword, the wealthy man's weapon, with its often elaborate and richly clad hilt and scabbard. It was designed, at any rate in the later period, for slashing and cutting rather than for stabbing. Its blade, about two feet six inches long, was of iron, with steel edges. An Anglo-Saxon warrior might have also the single-edged short sword called the *scramasax*, an axe either for chopping or for throwing, or a bow, a weapon rare in grave-finds but mentioned from time to time in the literature. Though he might be mounted, he would not normally fight on horse-

Warrior armed with spear, shield, sword and helmet

104

Riding to battle

back. His steed was for speedy transport when engaging highly mobile enemies like the Vikings.

The landowner's second major duty was that of building, reparing and manning fortresses. A text called the *Burghal Hidage* shows how this work was dealt out. The *Burghal Hidage* dates from the early tenth century when Edward the Elder was settling garrisons at strategic points of his kingdom to combat Danish attack. It lists 30 forts, and assesses each with reference to the number of hides of land which can maintain and man it. The calculation takes the form: 'For an acre's breadth of wall-setting and defence you need 16 hides. If each hide is represented by one man, then you can put four men to each pole of wall.' The assessment runs, 'to Hastings belong 500 hides, and to Lewes belong 1,200 hides, and to Burpham belong 720 hides, to Chichester belong 1,500 hides', and so on. This document (though it has several manifest errors) lists a total of over 25,000 hides, representing a substantial labour force. The work these people had to do varied according to the nature of the fortress they were assigned to, maintaining ancient ramparts or building new, and manning them in time of danger.

I deal in more detail with the work of construction in chapter IX below. Even when a stronghold was complete, the work was not over. Many were badly damaged by enemy action and would need extensive

'Building, repairing and manning fortresses'

repair. Others were improved, as at Lydford and Wallingford where stone walls strengthened the earlier earthen defences.

For the third duty, bridge-building, I quote a text in the

*Porchester castle, a Roman fort which the Anglo-Saxons
used as part of their burghal defence system*

Rochester cathedral records detailing the lands 'which must supply the labour' for keeping up the bridge at Rochester. The bridge had nine piers, each supporting three main cross-beams with planks over them. For maintenance purposes the piers with their linked beams were allotted among local land-owners. Starting from the east, the bishop took the first and third, the king the fourth, and the archbishop the fifth and ninth. Gillingham and Chatham looked after the second, Hollingbourn the sixth, and the people of Hoo the seventh and eighth. In the cases of the great landowners, king, bishop and archbishop, the document lists the particular estates from which they could call men to the work. 'The third pier again belongs to the bishop, and to provide planks for 2½ poles length and to fix three beams; from Halling, Trottiscliffe, Malling, Fleet, Stone, Pinden and Fawkham.'

All this work the king could count on getting done without cost to himself. But he needed subordinates to check that it was done properly, efficiently and to time, and also to ensure that his justice was upheld and his dues collected throughout his realm. These subordinates, his administrative officials, were the ealdormen, reeves and king's thanes. The extent of an ealdorman's authority varied in the different parts of the country. Sometimes he controlled a shire, sometimes several shires or even the lands of one of the ancient kingdoms. He was usually a man of family, wealthy in his own right, but he also held estates by virtue of his office, could claim rights of maintenance similar to those of the king, and probably had a *wergild* in respect of his office in addition to his personal one. The word reeve is imprecise, for there were several different sorts of reeves. As sheriff, shire-reeve, he could control a shire under an ealdorman. He could be a town-reeve, the king's representative in a borough. He could be a somewhat lesser official, in charge of a royal manor. The early meaning of the word 'thane', *thegn*, was 'servant', glossing Latin *assecula*. Thus the king's thane was the servant of the king, but a servant of high rank upholding the royal authority on his estate or at the king's court.

Chronicle entries stress the *fyrd*-duties of these three officials. In 860 'ealdorman Osric with the men of Hampshire and ealdorman Aethelwulf with the men of Berkshire fought against the Viking army and put it to flight'. Among the men killed with the Kentish army in 903 were ealdorman Sigewulf and ealdorman Sigehelm and the king's thane Ealdwold. In 1001 the Viking forces in the west country were opposed by 'Kola, the king's high-reeve, and Eadsige, the king's reeve, with what army they could gather'. When the men of Cambridge, deserted by their East Anglian colleagues, stood firm against the Danes in 1010, among those killed were the king's son-in-law Aethelstan, Oswig and his son, Wulfric, Eadwig, 'and many other good thanes and a countless number of people'.

The laws tell of their administrative duties, in some of which the diocesan bishop joined them. The ealdorman was the king's immediate representative in his executive area, acting as link

107

between king and people. Edgar's code promulgated 'at *Wihtbordesstan*', for instance, required that 'many copies be written from this one, and sent both to ealdorman Aelfhere [of Mercia] and ealdorman Aethelwine [of East Anglia], and they shall send them in all directions, so that this measure becomes known to poor and rich alike'. The ealdorman pronounced the king's peace in the meeting of the Five Boroughs of Nottingham, Leicester, Lincoln, Stamford and Derby. With the diocesan bishop he presided over the borough courts, held three times a year, and the shire courts, held twice, and there expounded the law. He kept an eye on the mutual relationships of those beneath him, examining a freeman who wished to change his lord, for example. He used his power to support those seeking justice or retribution in a blood-feud, and he was responsible for holding thieves.

The duties of reeve and thane overlapped with those of ealdorman. When an ealdorman controlled a large region, a reeve might exercise his authority within the individual shire. In the laws the reeve's recorded duties were to supervise trading and to administer justice. He witnessed the exchange of livestock and the purchase of goods, and he collected toll on transactions. He supervised the numbers of merchants going up country. He checked that there was no Sunday trading, and that people paid their church tithes. He kept an eye on the moneyers, and could be held responsible if there was any counterfeiting. As a judge he was enjoined to ensure justice, and to act without fear or favour. He presided at the people's meeting, initiated court proceedings, gave judgments, collected fines and took over property forfeited by criminals, arranged executions and ordeals, trailed stolen cattle and led the attack on kindred so strong that they defied common legal process. In many cases the king's thanes, too, had judicial powers which the king granted them, rights of private jurisdiction on their estates, and other general legal responsibilities, of serving on juries and seizing 'men who have often been accused, whom the reeve is proceeding against'. Yet the thanes' main duties were military and courtly. Alfred, so Asser says, divided them into three groups who served him in relays. Each group in turn lived a month at court, on duty night and day, and then spent the next two months at their homes, engaged in their private affairs. These would be the senior thanes, the *duguth*, but there would also be younger men, the *geoguth*, as yet unendowed with lands, who remained at court all the time, acting as the king's companions, courtiers and bodyguard.

When the king's authority was strong he exercised control over his officers, sometimes through the diocesan bishops. A reeve who disregarded royal ordinances was fined for disobedience, and the bishop exacted the fine. A reeve or thane who accepted a bribe lost his office. A judge who pronounced a false judgment—save through ignorance—paid compensation to the bishop and forfeited his thaneship. A reeve's judgments were witnessed by the bishop, who encouraged him to mercy in appropriate cases.

In return for his services the ealdorman—and presumably the reeve, too—held lands, was entitled to such privileges as fines for fighting in his presence and special rates of compensation for forcible entry into his hall, and took a proportion of the fines his courts exacted. The rest went to the king, and, together with tolls, forfeitures, inheritances and claims from the estates of foreigners, tribute from subject kings, money taken in return for privileges granted, gifts from other rulers, profits from dies issued to moneyers, and so on, made up his cash income. Asser tells that Alfred divided his annual revenue into two halves. Half went for religious and educational purposes, allotted to the poor, to the king's two monasteries, to a school, and to neighbouring religious houses in Wessex and Mercia. The other half he used for secular ends, a third going to the craftsmen from many races whom he gathered about him, a third to foreigners who visited him, and a third to the soldiers and thanes who served him at court. The soldiers here mentioned are the king's bodyguard, a small élite corps of professional fighting men, such as became famous under Cnut and the later Anglo-Saxon kings under their Scandinavian name 'house-carls'. The best list of serving thanes occurs in the will of the tenth-century king Eadred. He left 80 mancuses to each seneschal, keeper of the wardrobe and butler, 50 mancuses and five pounds in pence

Cupbearers

to each of the chaplains in charge of his relics, 30 mancuses to each steward, and minor bequests to other household officers. For the status of these servants, compare the bequests of 200 mancuses to the archbishop, and 120 to each diocesan bishop and ealdorman.

Many other people served the king, too, particularly in later times as administration became more complex. Alfred's division of his revenue shows that he must have had some accounting staff. The later Anglo-Saxon kings had secretaries and amanuenses for copying out royal laws and writs, recording grants and gifts. When the monetary system came under close royal control, the moneyers must have been important men, competent to guarantee purity and weight of metal, and employ workmen to make the coins, and the king himself must have had engravers who cut the official dies. Alfred, as Asser tells us, employed a number of bishops and chaplains, the priests Grimbald, John, Athelstan and Waerwulf, bishop Waerferth of Worcester and archbishop Plegmund, for marginally ecclesiastical purposes, reading to him and discussing religious texts, and helping with his translations, while Aethelred the Unready used archbishop Wulfstan to draft his law-codes.

Supporting him in matters of policy, law and taxation, and witnessing grants of land or privileges, the king had his council, his *witan, sapientes*, 'wise men'. These were the chief clerics, bishops and prominent abbots (or in pagan times the priests), and the leading laymen, ealdormen and thanes. Councils met at irregular intervals, often at the great church festivals. For instance, Athelstan issued a code of laws approved by 'the councillors who have been with me at Christmas at Exeter', while Edmund promulgated his first code after he had 'summoned a great synod of both clergy and laiety at London at holy Eastertide'. The preambles to other law-codes mention deliberation between the king and his advisers, so legal emendation and codification must have been primary duties of the council. In addition, the king talked over home and foreign policy with his *witan*. Edwin's council, held near Goodmanham, Yorkshire, debated whether to accept Christianity or reject it, and meetings of Aldfrith's, convened at Austerfield, Yorkshire, and Osred's, held at an unknown spot by the river Nidd, examined the case of the turbulent St Wilfrid. At Edwin's, the king asked each member in turn 'what he thought of this doctrine, previously unknown'. The councillors wanted to hear more about Christianity, and invited Paulinus to speak of his God. The missionary was so persuasive that Edwin acknowledged the true faith, and the chief priest of the old religion rode out to desecrate the pagan shrines. Bishops, abbots and the chief men of rank attended Osred's council at the Nidd. Archbishop Berhtwald and bishop Wilfrid opened proceedings by reading the Holy See's pronouncements on the latter's case, whereupon Berhtfrith, a high-ranking layman, asked for clarification of these obscure documents. The archbishop commented, and there was open discussion and indeed dispute. Then the bishops held a private conclave, finally agreeing with the laymen on a course of action. The chroniclers of Aethelred the Unready's reign held the king and his *witan* responsible for the direction of resistance to the Danes; it was they who decreed the assembly of warships at London in 992, the promise of tribute in 994, the use of naval and land forces in 999, truce and payment of *danegeld* again in 1002, 1006, 1011 and so on. The council's authority and acceptance would be needed to raise the tribute money promised.

The early king's councils, like the early kingdoms, were small and local. Thus, a seventh-century charter of king Hlothhere of Kent is witnessed by the king and 11 others, whose names, but not titles, are given. In contrast

King and council

A silver penny of king Athelstan. The obverse gives the royal name and the title REX TO *(tius)* B(*ritanniae*). *The reverse gives the moneyer's name and the mint-town, York*

are the great councils of later times. In their period of might in the eighth century the Mercian kings would sometimes assemble the archbishops and bishops of the whole southern province, together with the Mercian lay advisers. After Athelstan began to style himself *rex totius Britanniae*, 'king of all Britain', he held impressive meetings which brought together leading prelates and laymen from the whole of his dominions. Later kings continued the practice, though council members from the far north of the country seldom attended. When Aethelred the Unready granted land at Ardley, Oxfordshire, in the late tenth century, he had the document attested by archbishop Sigeric of Canterbury, 10 bishops from as far afield as Crediton, Lichfield and London, five ealdormen, 10 abbots and 13 king's thanes. Seventy council meetings are known from the tenth and eleventh centuries, and there may have been many more. These must have brought the king's servants scurrying across country to his court, lodging in official quarters or in tents on the way, and travelling in state, protected by the king's peace.

Further Reading

For the charters and writs, see the section 'Charters and Laws' in *English Historical Documents*, vol. 1, and for more detailed examination A. J. Robertson, *Anglo-Saxon Charters*; F. M. Stenton, *The Latin Charters of the Anglo-Saxon Period*; F. E. Harmer, *Anglo-Saxon Writs*. C. W. Hollister, *Anglo-Saxon Military Institutions on the Eve of the Norman Conquest*, describes the obligation to armed service in the later period, while D. M. Wilson, *The Anglo-Saxons*, has a chapter on 'Weapons and Warfare', and for greater detail there is H. R. E. Davidson, *The Sword in Anglo-Saxon England*. There is an account of the king's council at the end of the period in T. J. Oleson, *The Witenagemot in the Reign of Edward the Confessor*.

VIII

God's Thanes

In 597 St Augustine preached the Christianity of the Roman church before Aethelberht of Kent, and so forged the link with Rome which was to last till the Reformation. In 634 St Aidan founded a monastic centre at Lindisfarne, from which he taught the Northumbrians the Christianity of the Celtic church. The two Christianities were rivals, differing in teaching, organisation, practice and spirit. One had the Roman virtues of regularity, discipline, organisation and moderation; the other the Celtic ideals of asceticism, fervour, humility and piety. At the Synod of Whitby in 664 the Roman faction triumphed when the Northumbrian king Oswiu preferred the patronage of Peter, keeper of the keys of heaven, to Columba, father of the Celtic church. Yet Anglo-Saxon Christianity long retained Celtic traits. Even so pronounced a Romanist as Theodore, archbishop of Canterbury from 668 to 690, followed Celtic precedents in his reorganisation of the northern bishoprics. Contrariwise, even St Cuthbert, by temperament and education an adherent of Celtic Christianity, made his compromise with the dominant Roman form.

The differences between the two churches provide a useful opening to a discussion of their effects on Anglo-Saxon daily life. Typical of the Celtic was Aidan, monk of Iona, who became bishop of the Northumbrians and was at the same time abbot of Lindisfarne. Bede gives a glowing account of his character and way of life. He was discreet, kindly and generous, qualities that endeared him to the alien and heathen English. More typically Celtic, he was austere in his manner of life, abstinent, continent, humble, scholarly, and Bede contrasts his industry with the slothfulness of some of the clergy of his own day, scarcely a century later. Though a monk, he was not confined to his cloister but, in the Celtic manner, spent much of his life in pastoral travel through the north country, unlimited by diocesan boundaries. In humility he journeyed on foot unless his mission was urgent or his path hard. His companions were few, grave and pious. He owned 'nothing but his church and a few fields round it'. Of the material conditions of his life we know little, for the site of the Anglo-Saxon monastery of Lindisfarne is untraced, though it may lie beneath the grass of the inhospitable ridge called the Heugh, at the south end of Holy Island. The buildings were certainly meagre in the time of Aidan and his immediate successors. Bishop Finan put up a church 'in the Celtic manner, not of stone, but of hewn oak thatched with reeds'. When the Celtic brethren departed after their defeat at Whitby, they left few other buildings. 'They had no money but cattle.' Great men visited them solely to attend divine worship. If the king came, only five or six servants attended him. If he stayed on to dine, he got the plain food that the brethren ate. These men (as Bede admitted, even though he disapproved of their unorthodoxy) served God, not the world, and fed souls, not bellies. Consequently, all men held the religious life in high esteem.

The Celtic church must have been full of prelates like Aidan, enthusiastic in preaching and pastoral care, living their godly lives in simplicity. For instance, St Chad, bishop of Lichfield, answered with disarming humility Theodore's charge that he had not been properly consecrated in the Roman manner: he would be glad to give up episcopal office because he never thought himself worthy of it, and accepted it only under orders. Chad was another who travelled on foot to preach and minister. Theodore bade him take a horse whenever the way was long, but Chad was reluctant and Theodore had to push him on to its back with his own hands. Chad's comrade Owine (who had been head of queen Aethelthryth's household) 'forsook the things of this world, so that, giving up everything he had, dressed in a plain garment and carrying an axe and an adze in his hand, he came to . . . Lastingham, showing that he went to the monastery, not to live idle, but to toil'.

Contrasting with these is the intransigent figure of St Wilfrid, who championed the Roman cause at the Synod of Whitby, and became bishop of the Northumbrians and abbot of Hexham and Ripon. His biographer and follower, Eddius, ascribes to him most of the Christian virtues—veracity, piety, humility, learning, charity, righteousness, continence, diligence—all the qualities which the apostle Paul required in a bishop. He was habitually temperate, devoting himself to fasting, keeping vigil, reading and praying, and he took a daily cold bath, winter and summer. Eddius was a partial observer; the troubled course of Wilfrid's life shows that he was a man of stern character, a formidable and determined opponent, obstinate and convinced of his case, and a lover of the formal pomp of the Roman church. When Theodore deprived him of the see of York under admittedly obscure circumstances, he took his case to Rome and spent the rest of his life seeking reinstatement. His enemies charged Wilfrid with his 'temporal glory . . . his riches, the number of his monasteries, the greatness of the buildings, his countless army of followers in royal trappings and arms'.

Far from being content with few and humble buildings, he constructed at Ripon an elaborate church of stone. Kings, abbots, reeves and other dignitaries attended the consecration feast which lasted for three days, and they showed proper deference to the servants of God. At Hexham Wilfrid made a church on a scale not otherwise known on this side of the Alps. York Minster he rescued from the squalor it had fallen into, repaired and leaded the roof, glazed the

Wilfrid's crypt at Hexham

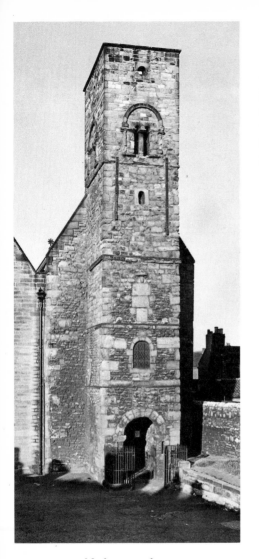

Monkwearmouth tower

windows, painted the walls and furnished the interior. Throughout his life Wilfrid watched over the worldly prosperity of his foundations, preserving them from encroachment. One of his last acts was to divide up his treasures, part to go to Rome, part to the abbots of Hexham and Ripon, part to those who had shared his troubled exile, and part to the poor for his soul's repose.

In recent years archaeologists have undertaken intensive excavation of two monasteries closely linked to the Roman cause, those of Wearmouth (Monkwearmouth) and Jarrow, which Benedict Biscop founded in 674 and 681. Benedict made several trips to Rome, became deeply influenced by its culture, and brought back with him books, relics, pictures, vestments and holy vessels. From Bede's *Lives of the Abbots* we know that he imported masons and glaziers from Gaul to build his church at Wearmouth in the Roman style. Excavation of the two sites confirms the technical sophistication of the workmanship. The walls were covered with fine plaster, some of which was painted. Plain and coloured glass filled the windows. Flooring was of red plaster, and roofs were leaded. At Monkwearmouth, there was decorative sculpture painted red or black. Jarrow at least seems to have had a planned and imposing set of buildings whose layout resembled those of the continental prototypes. The largest building yet found, probably a communal refectory, was 71 by 21 feet.

These monasteries were big. Together they held 600 monks in 716. Their early endowments of land comprised 70 and 40 hides respectively. From Rome Benedict brought a cantor who taught methods of chanting and introduced the Roman order of services. The books he collected formed the bases of libraries which were to bring his two houses to the forefront of learning— Bede, who worked most of his life at Jarrow, had access to a splendid collection of classical and patristic texts, Christian poetry and historical and hagiographical works. Benedict studied the monastic life in 17 old foundations, and by judicious selection prepared a rule for his own communities. The whole enterprise was an ambitious attempt to bring formal monasticism to northern England, to bring the regular life—life lived according to a *regula*—and to link the teaching and ritual of the English church firmly to those of Rome.

In contrast stand the finds at Whitby, where was the great monastery of *Streoneshalh*. The site is large and its history complex, but at least seven of the early buildings were traced, free-standing and grouped with no obvious attempt at planning. They were of stone, and the absence of tile or slate fragments shows they were thatched. One of them was a large communal building, possibly a guest-house or store. Two, of similar pattern, were rectangular, 18 by 11 feet, with hearth and drain. The disposition suggests that each was internally divided into two rooms, one perhaps for living, the other for sleeping; these look like individual cells for inmates. Thus this monastery was probably a complex of separate living huts with a communal church and other buildings ('both public and private', as Bede says of Coldingham), such as the hospital where the poet Caedmon was taken to die. It is likely that there was a fence running round the site (like the great thorn hedge at St Wilfrid's monastery of Oundle), protecting the community and dividing it from the world outside.

The pattern for this type of monastery was Celtic. Clearly there is a relationship between the house made up of a group of separate cells, and the hermitage with the single cell

King Athelstan presents a book to the community of St Cuthbert

surrounded by an enclosing wall. Though the monks and nuns of Whitby, Lindisfarne, Coldingham and so on followed monastic rules no less than did those of Wearmouth and Jarrow, the emphasis was less on the ordered life of the community and on the ritual of the church, less even on learning, and more upon the ascetic and pastoral lives. Such a monastery might have, among its inmates, a bishop who came under the abbot's authority, but whose life involved long journeys, preaching, baptising, confirming and visiting the isolated country communities. Such a man was St Cuthbert, whose austere life was written by Bede and by an anonymous monk of Lindisfarne. Cuthbert was a man of importance. He was prior of Melrose and subsequently of Lindisfarne, and became bishop of the Northumbrians, first at Hexham and then at Lindisfarne. Yet his instincts were those of a hermit, and at times he withdrew from public life and became an anchorite on Farne. Bede describes Cuthbert's cell on that island. It had a high, circular, surrounding wall, four or five poles in diameter and built of rocks and turf. Within were two buildings, an oratory and a dwelling, with dug-out floors and plank walls, roofed with rough timber and thatch. He had a well, and a little garden which he sowed with barley, since wheat would not grow in the poor soil.

In withdrawing into isolation like this, Cuthbert was not being eccentric. Farne was a popular place for hermits. Aidan had preceded Cuthbert there, and a priest called Aethelwald succeeded to the cell. As bishop of Hexham, St John of Beverley used to retire to a house surrounded by a wood and dyke, and there live with few companions. When the sub-king Oethilwald wanted a monastery to retire to for prayer and thought, bishop Cedd chose for it the site of Lastingham, 'among high and distant mountains, which looked more like lurking-places for robbers and dens for wild beasts than dwellings for men'. There through Lent Cedd lived alone, cleansing the place by

The isolated Farne Islands where Cuthbert had his hermit's cell

prayer and by fasting 'till evening, when he took no more sustenance than a little bread, one hen's egg, and a little milk mixed with water'. The hermit Hereberht lived on an island in Derwentwater still called St Herbert's Isle. At Crowland, amid the fens, St Guthlac built a tiny hut over a plundered barrow. There he stayed solitary, wearing clothes of skin, eating nothing until sunset and wrestling with demons.

As a bishop Cuthbert clearly kept some state. A sizeable retinue (*comitatus*) accompanied his pastoral journeys. Abbesses and men of rank received him with honour. The town reeve of Carlisle showed him the local sights. He mixed with royalty. Yet his anonymous biographer insists that he retained his 'humility of heart and poverty of dress . . . maintaining the dignity of a bishop without abandoning the ideal of a monk or the virtue of a hermit'. Cuthbert's austere life was widely known and much praised. He wearied himself by watching through the nights in prayer and psalm-singing, sometimes immersing himself in the sea up to the waist or even the neck in self-mortification. He worked with his hands to keep awake. He wore plain clothing, and seldom changed his boots.

Celtic and Roman houses alike admired the simple life, though not necessarily in the same degree. Descriptions of early Anglo-Saxon monasticism recount the duty of manual labour such as Owine and Cuthbert took upon themselves. Even monks of high birth, the sources stress, accepted it. Ceolfrith, who became abbot of Jarrow, and Eosterwine, who ruled Monkwearmouth, were both of noble family. For a time Ceolfrith acted as the monastery baker, sieving flour, lighting and clearing out the oven and preparing bread. Eosterwine took his share in winnowing and grinding, milking, baking, gardening, working in the kitchen, ploughing and toiling at the

Fragments of St Cuthbert's portable altar recovered from his tomb.
An inscription records the dedication in honour of St Peter

A page from the Lindisfarne gospels

forge, continuing these humble tasks even after his election as abbot. Some monks become highly skilled. Aethelwulf's poem *De Abbatibus* mentions a brother Cwicwine, a trained smith, who made metal vessels for the cell. The magnificent *Lindisfarne Gospels* manuscript was written by Eadfrith, bishop of Lindisfarne, and bound by Aethelwald, his successor in that office, 'as he well knew how to'. An anchorite called Billfrith decorated its case [? made a case for it] adding gold, silver and gems.

In humanity's fallen state, discipline of this order was hard to keep up. Even in the seventh century some establishments were slack. For example, in 679, Coldingham monastery 'was burnt by divine fire'. Bede tells why. Some time earlier a conscientious Celt called Adamnan had a vision which threatened the house with destruction because 'the cells that were built for praying and reading are now converted into places of feasting, drinking, talking and other delights'. When he passed the warning on, the inmates improved for a while, but relapsed into their bad ways and were destroyed by God's avenging flame. Bede himself complained to archbishop Ecgbert of the number of Northumbrian houses 'allowed the name of monasteries . . . but having nothing at all of the monastic way of life'. These were often estates which their owners had converted into monasteries to escape paying royal dues, while they themselves continued to live in lay fashion. Of St Cuthbert's manner of dress Bede comments that it was very ordinary, neither fine nor slovenly, adding, 'his example is followed in the same monastery to the present day, so that nobody has clothing of varied or costly colour, since they are quite satisfied with those which natural sheeps' wool supplies'. Yet tradition says that, a few years later, in 737 or 738 when king Ceolwulf of Northumbria joined the monks of Lindisfarne, he persuaded them to some relaxation of strictness. When the Vikings sacked the monastery in 793 Alcuin wrote to the survivors tactfully enquiring if there had been any fault in their behaviour, and exhorting them to sobriety of life and simplicity of clothing.

So far I have dealt with early monasticism largely in Northumbria. There is some excuse for this, for that region was culturally very important in the seventh century, and had many religious houses, as Abercorn, Whithorn, Coquet Island, Tynemouth, Hackness, Hartlepool and Gilling. But there were many also scattered through the other Anglo-Saxon kingdoms, in places like Partney, Peterborough, Ely, Brixworth, Repton, Barking, Woking, Bermondsey, Chertsey, Canterbury, Dover, Lyminge, Reculver, Wimborne, Nursling, Malmesbury, Glastonbury and Bradford on Avon. Some were double monasteries, containing nuns and monks living under the rule of an abbess. Such was the great house of Whitby, controlled in its heyday by the formidable Hild, kinswoman of king Oswiu of Northumbria, and others were Hartlepool, Coldingham, Barking, Wimborne and Bardney. In general the Celtic influence was stronger in the north, the Roman predominating in the south, but there are exceptions to this generalisation. The Irishman Fursa founded a community in Suffolk, which was later ruled by his brother Foilan. The place-name Malmesbury (*Mealdelmes byrig*) contains a conflation of two personal names, of the Irish Maildubh who set up the religious house there and the West Saxon Aldhelm, his pupil, who became its most famous son. A surviving description of the seventh-century monastery of Abingdon suggests a disposition of the Celtic type: a church, 12 cells set round it in a circle for 12 monks to live, eat and sleep in, and round that again a high protective wall.

The English monasteries, strong at the beginning of the eighth century, had declined by its end, and they virtually vanished during the ninth, partly as a result of ferocious Viking attack. In the tenth century were established, or re-established, the great houses of later Anglo-Saxon and medieval times: Glastonbury, Abingdon, Winchester, Winchcombe, Chertsey, Ramsey, Evesham, Peterborough, Ely, Thorney, Crowland and many others. This was a more conscious programme of monastic foundation than the earlier one had been. Great men led it: king Edgar himself, St Dunstan of Glastonbury, Worcester, London and Canterbury, St Aethelwold of Abingdon and Winchester, St Oswald of Worcester and York. There was a close link with the revived Benedictinism of the

St Dunstan kneels before Christ

123

continent, and the monks of these new foundations lived largely according to the Benedictine rule. A conference held in the later part of Edgar's reign led to the compilation of the *Regularis concordia*, an agreed form of ritual and discipline for English monasteries deriving its material from traditional Benedictine teaching, from the reformed French and Lotharingian houses, notably Fleury, and from 'the honourable tradition of this country of ours'.

King Alfred divided a king's subjects into three groups, 'those who pray, and soldiers and workmen'. To the homilist Aelfric, who was monk at Cerne Abbas, Dorset, in 987, and

'Those who pray'

abbot of Eynsham in 1005, these three, the *laboratores*, *bellatores* and *oratores*, were the three supports of the throne; the *oratores* are 'those who intercede for us to God, promoting Christianity among Christian peoples in the service of God as spiritual toil, being devoted solely to that for the benefit of us all'. As defined in the *Regularis concordia*, the formal life of the monastery was a life for 'those who pray'. The ritual varied from season to season, and indeed from day to day, for the year's variation in climate and lighting and the church's annual pattern of celebration and mourning governed the monk's timetable. There were three seasons, Easter to 13 September, 14 September to the beginning of Lent, and the six weeks of Lent itself. Times would be less precise than ours, each day having three ascertainable points, sunrise, noon and sunset. In summer a monk would get up at about 1.30 a.m., take his first meal (*prandium*) at noon, his second (*cena*) at about 5.30, and go to bed in the common dormitory at about 8.15. Into his waking hours he would have to fit the night office (Nocturns, the modern Matins, at 2.0 a.m.) and the seven day hours, Matins (the modern Lauds) at daybreak, Prime at 6.0 a.m., Tierce at 8.0, Sext at 11.30, None at 2.30 p.m., Vespers at about 6.0 and Compline at 8.0. There were many additional daily services: offices of All Saints and of the Dead, the *trina oratio* or threefold prayer for his own in-

Regularis Concordia. *Edgar sits between Dunstan and Aethelwold, and the three hold a scroll representing the agreed code of monastic law. Below, bound by the rule, kneels a monk*

tentions, for the king, queen and benefactors, and for the faithful departed, the Gradual and Penitential Psalms, psalms for the royal house, the litanies, the daily Morrow and High Masses, as well as private prayer, masses and confession, and daily attendance at chapter where the martyrology and rule were read, and where sinners publicly admitted their faults. After Matins and *prandium* there might be short periods of rest or meditation, and there was a total of five hours spent in intellectual or physical work between Tierce and Sext and between None and Vespers. In winter the monks had more sleep, getting up at about 2.30 and going to bed at 6.30. There was a slightly different order of services, and only one meal,

125

Bronze censer-cover from Pershore

cena, eaten at about 2.0 p.m., with a drink served to them in the evening. Lent had only one meal a day, taken at about 4.30 p.m. It was a frugal one, devoid of fats and at times even of milk and eggs. The *Concordia* gives details of the special services and practices on feast and holy days. These were elaborate and ceremonious with, for example, the washing of the pavement of the church, of the altars, and of the feet of 'as many poor men as the abbot shall have provided for' on Maundy Thursday, and a re-enacting of the three women seeking Christ's body in the sepulchre on Easter Day.

Some of the monks held official positions. At the head of a house was the abbot, usually elected from among the inmates, supported by the king's consent. Others, his assistants in the general running of the establishment, were the dean (*decanus*), provost (*praepositus*) and prior. The sacrist controlled the church and its services. The master looked after the children under training for the monastic life. The cantors were in charge of choral services and took special singing duties. The *circa* was responsible for discipline, rebuking the idle, vain, untidy or sleepy. Each day monks were appointed to cook and serve meals, and a lector read improving texts in the refectory while his fellows fed. These had the benefit of an extra snack at mid-morning, since they would not get their midday meal until everyone else had finished. For five hours on ordinary days the monks would do the work which the Benedictine rule required. This was often intellectual, and would include study, writing and the preparation of the superb manuscripts for which the scriptoria of Christ Church, Canterbury, and Winchester became famous. Though there is little evidence of it from late Anglo-Saxon sources, many may have done rough manual work, but probably not heavy field or garden labour. Aelfric's

Life of St Aethelwold shows monks working side by side with lay masons on the restoration of their church, and also preparing meals for the builders. On the site of Glastonbury abbey archaeologists have traced dome-topped furnaces and crucibles used for making glass, as well as glass fragments, and have linked them to the late Anglo-Saxon monastery.

The children of the cloister, the *schola*, provided most of the recruits to the monasteries. They had a slightly easier time for they were allowed more sleep and took their meals earlier in the day. The master (*magister* or *custos scholae*) watched over them, under fairly precise rules framed in the *Concordia*. It is interesting to note a number of provisions to prevent homosexual attachments between them and the grown-ups. Monks are forbidden to 'embrace or kiss, as it were, youths or children; let their affection for them be spiritual, let them keep from words of flattery, and let them love the children reverently and with the greatest circumspection'. No monk, even the master himself, should be alone with a boy; a third person must always be present. Despite this clear care for their welfare, the boys led an austere life. Aelfric's *Colloquy* contains a short account of a typical day. Asked what he has done so far that day, the boy replies, 'A lot of things. During the night, when I heard the bell, I got out of my bed, went to church and sang Nocturns with the brethren. Then we sang the office of All Saints and Matins, after that Prime and the seven psalms with the litanies and the chapter mass; then Tierce and the mass of the day. After that we sang Sext [Old English *middæg*, "midday"] and ate, drank and slept. Then we got up and sang None. And *now* we are here in your presence ready to hear what you tell us,'—that is, they are in school during the afternoon work period. The questioner asks if the lad has had a beating that day, presumably for error or laxness in the services, and he replies, 'No, because I was wary.' The lad is asked what he had to eat. 'I still eat meat, because I am a child subject to the rod.' Otherwise he eats 'vegetables, eggs, fish, cheese, butter, beans and all clean things', but denies that he is a glutton. He drinks ale if he can get it, otherwise water. He cannot afford wine which is in any case 'a drink for old and wise ones, not for the young and silly'.

*The monks of Canterbury, obedient
to St Benedict's rule*

He sleeps in the common dormitory, and is woken either by the bell or the master's rod.

The life the *Concordia* formulates was a busy but quiet one, devoted to such virtues as frugality, obedience, humility and charity. The boy's comment on his dinner suggests that many monks had a meatless diet, and St Aethelwold is said to have eaten the flesh of animals or birds during one three-month period only, when Dunstan ordered it for his health's sake, and again in his final illness. There was usually some relaxation of strictness for the sick, and a general lightening in winter. For instance, the brethren were allowed 'a fire as long as necessity demands and excessive cold lasts'. Ideally the monastery was a peaceful place. During parts of the day and in some parts of the house the rule of absolute silence applied. Otherwise monks could speak on necessary matters of business or study, but in hushed voices. The *Concordia* stresses 'the merit of obedience'. Nobody should act in any way as though of his own will, nor, 'puffed up with overweening pride, . . . do the least thing without the prior's permission'. At the Christmas vigil and on Easter Day, the brethren, 'with lowly devotion', beg pardon of the abbot (representing Christ) for their many failings. The abbot forgives them, and then, prostrate on the ground, himself asks their pardon. The children, monks and abbot took their turns in the daily duty of the Maundy, following their Lord's example at the Last Supper. In a specially appointed place they washed the feet of three poor men 'chosen from those who are customarily fed in the monastery', and gave them the same

The maundy

meal as the monks were having. Poor travellers got the same humble service, and were supplied with food to take on their way. This was an ideal of life, calm, ordered and virtuous. Naturally there were backsliders, like the thief Edwin whom St Aethelwold punished by binding his hands with a curse.

In its elaboration the *Concordia* seems intended for large and flourishing monasteries, highly organised in ritual and discipline, with choirs that could be divided up for antiphonal singing. Certainly many of the later Anglo-Saxon monasteries were wealthy and probably splendid, so that they could hold impressive services. What comes as a surprise, however, is to learn how small some, even of the most famous, were. In 1040 New Minster, Winchester, had about 40 monks. On the eve of the Norman Conquest Evesham and Worcester had only 12 each. Shortly after the Conquest Durham had 23, Gloucester 11, Abingdon 28, and Christ Church, Canterbury, about 60.

It is misleading to equate the Anglo-Saxon church, as I have done hitherto, with the monasteries. Not all priests were monks, nor all monks priests. Yet the monasteries played an impressive part in introducing and spreading Christianity. When they were strong they filled the bishoprics of England with their members. Many diocesan centres—Canterbury, Winchester, Worcester, Sherborne, Lindisfarne, Hexham, for example— were monastic, and here the bishop was normally one of the monks, sometimes elected by the brethren themselves. Of the 116 bishops consecrated between 960 and 1066 67 are known to have been monks, and only 14 were certainly secular priests. The daily life of the secular clergy is poorly recorded, for there are many gaps in our knowledge of parish and diocesan organisation. King Edgar's code (II and III Edgar) distinguishes three types of church: an 'old minster', entitled to the tithes from a thane's demesne and from his tenants' land as it is ploughed up, as well as traditional church dues; a church with a graveyard built by a thane on his own land, which receives only a third part of the thane's own tithe; a church without a graveyard, getting no tithe but endowed from the thane's remaining income. Aethelred's eighth code distinguishes four types, defined by the penalty payable for violating their rights of sanctuary: a chief minster (five pounds), a lesser minster (120 shillings—two pounds), a small church with a cemetery (60 shillings), and a field-church (30 shillings).

The chief minster was presumably a cathedral church, the bishop's seat. The bishop was at all times the primary pastoral figure in his diocese, and in the early period and in the huge northern regions he bore the brunt of the work of teaching, baptising and catechising, as well as confirming. Bede's description of Cuthbert's episcopacy stresses his visits to remote and mountainous districts seldom approached by other teachers. In the eighth century a letter from Bede to archbishop Ecgbert of York suggests that the diocesan organisation was very primitive: 'And since the distances between places under your diocesan control are too great for you alone to be able to cross them all, preaching the word of God in the different villages and homesteads, even in the course of a whole year, it is very necessary for you to appoint assistants in your sacred work by ordaining priests and instituting teachers, who can devote themselves to preaching the word of God in the various villages, celebrating the holy mysteries, and especially performing the rites of holy baptism.' By the end of the tenth century when abbot Aelfric and archbishop Wulfstan were writing on the nature of the church, the bishop seems more of an official directing an organisation. He is *Godes bydel*, 'God's herald', and is to the people as the shepherd to the flock. He must carry out his priestly tasks, in saying his hours, preaching, praying, giving alms, performing the Maundy; and he must teach, learn, read and correct books. He ought also to have some handicraft, since this serves to prevent idleness and so temptation. He must obey Christian teaching, and beware of such sins as pride and gluttony, and such vanities as hunting and hawking, which bring his rank into disrepute. He must fear God, but not any worldly power. But there are also specific administrative and episcopal duties. He attends folk-meetings, where his authority can ensure conciliation. He supervises ordeals and oath-takings, checks legal rights and examines legal measures. He adjudicates in disputes between priests in his diocese. He has the particular responsibility of examining candidates for the priesthood, ensuring that they have an adequate knowledge of doctrine, ritual and penitential law, and enough mathematics

Consecrating a church

to enable them to work out the church's year correctly. If there is a serious shortage of priests, he may accept a *samlæred*, 'half-learned', man, provided that the candidate gives sureties that he will continue his studies after ordination. The bishop ordains to the priesthood, and to the six lower orders of clerks, giving to each his symbol of office. In his own diocese he must visit and examine his clergy, enquire into abuses and convene local synods. On a national level he must attend the great synods of the church. For example, at the Synod of Hertford in 673 there were present archbishop Theodore, bishops Putta of Rochester, Bisi of East Anglia, Leuthere of Wessex and Wynfrid of Mercia, and 'many other teachers of the church'. St Wilfrid was absent, but sent his proctors. This synod dealt with 'necessary affairs of the church', and made decrees as to the proper observance of Easter, the authority of bishops, the place of monks and clerks and Christian marriage. It further arranged that 'we should meet once a year, on 1 August, at the place called *Clofeshoh*'.

As an important subject a bishop would be a member of the king's council. One of his tasks would be to attest charters and grants, and indeed these witness lists are essential guides to episcopal succession in some cases. As the head of a community that might own large estates from which it derived its main income, he must be something of a business man and lawyer. A report from the Synod of Brentford in 781 shows bishop Hathored of Worcester negotiating with the powerful king Offa of Mercia a settlement of a dispute about possession of land. St Oswald of Worcester reorganised the management of his community's vast estates. The wealth of extant documents from his episcopacy includes over 70 leases which show him letting out estates for the lifetimes of the original lessees and two successive heirs in return for services and dues.

A bishop could be a rich man as surviving wills show. The tenth-century Theodred of London, for example, left a number of estates mainly in East Anglia to church communities like St Paul's, London, Mendham, Hoxne, Glastonbury and Bury St Edmunds, bequeathed land to relatives and to his lord, made various charitable gifts and freed numbers of men for the good of his soul, and disposed of a variety of lesser objects, including two silver cups, two chalices, four horses, two swords, four

Bishop Oswald of Worcester leases land at Teddington and Alstone, Gloucs., for a period of three lives

shields, four spears, two massbooks, various vestments and relics and a total of 250 marks of gold. In the early eleventh century archbishop Aelfric of Canterbury left estates to the abbeys of Christ Church, Canterbury, Abingdon, Cholsey and St Albans, land to his sisters and their children, his best ship and tackle together with 60 helmets and 60 mailcoats to his lord, a ship to the people of Kent and the same to the people of Wiltshire (to help them meet their obligations to supply ships to the king), books and a tent to St Albans abbey, a pectoral cross, ring and psalter to archbishop Wulfstan of York, and a crucifix to bishop Aelfheah of Winchester. Debts owed him by the peoples of Kent, Middlesex and Surrey he forgave. Bishops of this wealth might need Wulfstan's warning 'not to give too much heed to worldly pomp or vain ostentation'.

Bronze seal-die of bishop Aethelwald of East Anglia

Of the priests' lives we know less. The minsters, great and lesser, were non-monastic churches, holding authority over larger areas than the later parishes, and served by groups of priests. Often such priests were encouraged to live together very like monks, save that they were not bound to a rule. Thus they might provide communal church services, live in community with a common refectory and dormitory, and hold the church income in common. Arrangements like these appeared at different times in different churches. York, it seems, had some such organisation as early as the seventh century, and it certainly continued there in the eleventh, when it was found, too, in Southwell and Beverley. The secular canons whom king Edgar expelled from the Old and New Minsters, Winchester, and from Chertsey and Milton Abbas in 964 were presumably priests of this sort. Aelfric's *Life of St Aethelwold* describes the Winchester clergy as 'evil-living clerics' who had married unlawfully, and were 'given over to gluttony and drunkenness', but Aelfric was a professed monk, unlikely to be objective in his description.

The church income came partly from the endowments and bequests of pious benefactors, and partly from the church dues which freemen paid. By the early eleventh century these were plough-alms 15 days after Easter, tithe of young beasts by Whitsun, tithe of the crops by All Saints' Day, church-scot by St Martin's Day, and light-dues three times a year, as well as Peter's pence (*Romfeoh*, 'Rome-money', since this was sent to Rome) by St Peter's Day. Tithe did not remain absolutely in the church's possession. According to Wulfstan it must be divided into three parts, one-third to go to the poor and to pilgrims, one-third for repair and upkeep of the church, and one-third to God's servants working there.

In the smaller church the priest's position was less secure financially. If we are to believe Edgar's laws such churches were usually put up by local landowners, and there is evidence to show that the builders and their successors sometimes regarded them very much as their own property (like heathen temples in earlier times), and as sources of income like, say, a mill was. Presumably the church had an endowment of land when it was established, but it would be less likely to attract gifts thereafter than the 'old minsters', and it had few rights to church dues. A priest at one of these churches was much at his lord's mercy, and Domesday Book makes clear that, by the end of the Anglo-Saxon period, village priests differed widely in wealth. On the other hand, the priest's social position was clear. In a revealing comment on class relationships, Wulfstan wrote: 'See, it often happens that a slave gets his freedom from a *ceorl*, and that through an earl's grace a *ceorl* becomes worthy of a thane's rank, and through the king's grace a thane becomes worthy of an earl's. It is evil, then, if one who rises to holy orders and to the rank of God's thane through God's grace and divine learning, should not be thought worthy of respect and security in the world's eyes.' He points out that a singer could become a priest and a scribe a bishop, for God's teaching shows a shepherd, David, elevated to the kingship, and a fisherman, Peter, made bishop. Within the church the highborn should not despise the low. The moral is clear. 'Rightly understood, all men are of the same birth', and priests have a common social position. Since they are *weofodthegnas*, 'altar-thanes', this is the thane's rank. Certainly legislation links priest and thane. According to a law of Aethelred, 'If an altar-thane orders his life rightly [that is, remains celibate] according to the teaching of the books, then he is entitled to the full *wergild* and dignity of a thane, both in life and the grave.'

Further Reading

C. J. Godfrey, *The Church in Anglo-Saxon England*, covers the whole Christian period, while more limited studies are A. Hamilton Thompson, *Bede, his Life, Times and Writings*; E. S. Duckett, *Alcuin, Friend of Charlemagne*; and the same writer's *Saint Dunstan of Canterbury*. The monastic life is described in D. Knowles, *The Monastic Order in England*, and there is an edition and translation of the *Regularis Concordia* by T. Symons.

IX

King's Hall, Peasant's Cottage, Town House

Little remains of the homes of the Anglo-Saxons. This is not surprising for they were largely made of perishable materials. Their walls, foundations and supports were of wood, and their floors often of earth, sometimes sanded, though they could be of chalk, stones, flints or animal bones. Often all that survives of a house is the marks still visible in the ground of holes that were once filled with beams, planks or sills, and such things are hard to find and hard to identify. Spotting a cemetery is comparatively easy, and so hundreds have been excavated, often in part only. But finding a settlement site takes skill and application, and they are correspondingly little known. Only in recent years have the advancing techniques of air photography and of excavation brought to light quite large numbers of settlement sites. Even when a site is known, it takes a skilled excavator to find, identify and interpret the post-holes, to visualise from the marks in the earth what sort of structure stood above it, to distinguish between successive buildings occupying the same site, to determine the relationship between individual buildings in a complex. And when that is done there is the equally important problem of relating the settlement to the countryside in which it was set, of seeing the house in its economic context.

Until recent years our knowledge of Anglo-Saxon houses was derived largely from literary sources, and these are still important, though they are often imprecise and sometimes of uncertain validity. Revealing is the famous annal 755 in the *Chronicle*, already mentioned. It tells in detail of the killing of king Cynewulf of Wessex by Cyneheard, brother of the deposed king Sigebriht. Cynewulf was visiting his mistress at her home, a fortified manor. At the moment of attack they were occupying together a private building called a *bur*, 'bower', and the small retinue that had accompanied the king were some distance away, apparently in another building, probably asleep and certainly unprepared. The complex of buildings must have been protected by a palisade or rampart with a gate in it which could be barred, but which seems to have been left open. At any rate, the avenging Cyneheard and his men managed to get in, attack the *bur* and kill the king, despite his gallant defence. The king's men knew nothing of the onset until they heard the woman's cries. They seized their arms and rushed, each as he got ready, to the scene of the slaying, where Cyneheard tried to buy their support. They refused and were cut down. Cyneheard barricaded himself in the manor by closing the outer gates, and there, next morning, he was besieged by the rest of the king's men who had spent the night some way off. After a fruitless parley they stormed the fort, putting its defenders to the sword. The chronicler is eager to relate this dramatic tale. He is concerned with the incidents and, assuming we know what sort of house he is talking about, omits to describe it. Yet the nature of the events tells us something of the house plan. There must have been a surrounding wall, presumably defensive. Within it were several buildings, some distance apart, with individual functions; one is named, the lady's private chamber, another is implied, the main hall where the king's men ate and slept, and by the nature of things there must have been others, a kitchen, stables, storehouses, latrines and so on.

Other written sources give general confirmation to these surmises. The house occupied by Cynewulf's mistress was obviously one of some consequence. The heroic poem *Beowulf* tells of another great dwelling, the hall built for king Hrothgar. Admittedly, *Beowulf* is a poem, not a history. Admittedly, too, the action takes place in Denmark and Sweden, not England, and at an early date, *c.* 500. But the poem which survives is an English one, and the descriptions derive something from English models. The king's hall, which has the royal name *Heorot*,

'Hart', is a place of splendour. It is tall and gabled, of timber clamped with iron, approached by a paved path and apparently entered by double doors. Externally it is lavishly decorated, the roof gleaming with gold, whatever that may mean. Inside, the walls are covered with tapestries which also shine with gold. The floor is of stone, apparently variegated. Seats or benches line the walls, fixed somehow or other to the ground-sill, and these again are 'adorned with gold', perhaps having coverings embroidered with gold thread. Here the men dine, and here they sleep on beds and mattresses, their weapons ready to hand in case of sudden attack. But outside the hall and some distance away are other lodgings for which the term *bur* is used. We know little about them, save that they are of wood, and perhaps have wooden floors. They are private chambers, occupied by the king and queen and their most important retainers. And, when the great hall was subjected to continuous nightly attack from the monster Grendel, there was, as the poet sardonically remarks, 'no difficulty in finding men who sought their couches a bit farther off among the "bowers". . . . Anyone who escaped the fiend afterwards kept himself farther away and safer.'

Minor sources, in themselves small and insignificant, add to the picture. The heroic fragment *The Fight at Finnesburh* tells how a regiment of Danes held the two doors of a wooden hall against a Frisian army until, after five days' fighting, a truce was cobbled up. When Edwin of Northumbria was deliberating over accepting Christianity, one of his advisers compared man's life in this world, bounded at either end by the unknown, to 'the quick flight of a sparrow through the hall where you sit at supper with your thanes and ministers in the winter. There is a good fire in the midst, while outside storms of rain and snow are raging. The sparrow, flying in at one door and straight out at the other, is safe from the wintry storm whilst he is inside, but after an instant of fine weather he quickly vanishes out of sight into the dark night from which he came'. The wall-hangings and seat-covers of *Beowulf* are confirmed by bequests in wills: one Wulfwaru, of whom nothing else is known, had several wall-hangings or tapestries, for she

Harold feasts in an upper room at his manor house at Bosham

left one to St Peter's monastery, Bath, a hanging for a hall to her elder son Wulfmaer, and one for a hall and another for a *bur* to her second son Aelfwine, while the tenth-century Wynflaed left to Eadgifu a long and a short hall-tapestry and three seat-coverings, and also disposed of other tapestries less carefully defined. The typical wooden structure of this later time is defined in an extended metaphor from a learned prose work called Byrhtferth's *Manual*. Comparing the educational process to that of building a house Byrhtferth commented: 'First of all the house site is surveyed, then the timber is cut, the ground-sills neatly fitted together, the beams laid, the rafters fastened to the ridge-piece and supported with braces, and then the house is elegantly decorated.' A *Chronicle* entry for 978 shows that some houses had more than one storey, for in that year an upper floor collapsed, and 'the leading councillors of England fell down . . . all but the holy archbishop Dunstan who remained alone, standing on a beam'. A letter to king Edward the Elder dealing with the legal ownership of an estate shows the private nature of the *bur*, which could yet be used for official business. It tells how Alfred the Great had given judgment in an interview he held as 'the king stood washing his hands within the *bur* at Wardour'. Finally, the diversity of buildings within the one complex, the royal or nobleman's seat, is confirmed in a passage written by Alfred himself. In translating into English the *Soliloquies* of St Augustine, the king often expanded his original by adding references or allusions drawn from his own experience. In one such he compared the diversity of ways by which a man could achieve wisdom to the variety of circumstances under which he may live within the precincts of the royal palace, 'some in the *bur*, some in the hall, some on the threshing-floor, some in prison, and yet they all live by the grace of the same lord'.

This gives a descending series of social ranks, from lord to retainer, workman and felon, for the nobleman's hall combined the characteristics of home, fortress, farm, workshop, administrative centre and, as we shall see, church. Alfred's comment is welcome, for excavators have recently explored one of the royal manors of the kings of Wessex, at Cheddar in Somerset. Literary sources had pointed to its existence, and a rescue dig, anticipating the building of a new school, produced material details which link happily with Alfred's remarks. The site is complex, in continuous use from Anglo-Saxon to modern times, and the interpretation correspondingly hard. Dr P. A. Rahtz, who directed the excavation, isolated ninth-, tenth- and eleventh-century features, revealing the development of a royal residence over many years. To the north of the two-acre site was cut a long ditch to drain away storm water. By the tenth century the eastern boundary had its own ditch, some three feet deep, and bearing on its inner bank a fence with traces of the standing timbers of a double gate, and perhaps also a flagstaff or pole for carrying a trophy. In the ninth

A reconstruction of the royal estate at Cheddar

century there were at least three important buildings on the site. The main one, running north–south, was a long hall, 78 feet long and with bellying sides 20 feet apart at the widest. The structure was of closely set posts, each about nine inches square, set in trenches, and there were also signs of inner posts which may have held an upper floor. The two main entrances were at the middles of the long sides, and seem to have opened into internal porches. Further inside and nearer the south wall was a spread of burnt clay suggesting an open fire. Some sort of fencing with an entrance on the west side surrounded the hall. There were two smaller buildings, 25 by 14 feet and 30 by 24 feet, the latter with inner post-holes which could have supported looms or fixed benches. The buildings did not last long, for by the tenth century the site held quite a different group. Gone was the long hall, and on part of its plot stood a small building, ?22 by 14 feet, which is identified as a chapel since later chapels covered this area. The main hall had different proportions from its ninth-century predecessor, being 60 by 28–30 feet, running east–west, with entrances at the two ends. It was built of massive posts, up to two feet square and set at eight-foot intervals, the spaces presumably filled with ground timbers and plank walling. There were several other small buildings, including one of curious shape, a central circular area linked to diametrically set rectangular cellars, one of which contained traces of a fire. The walls of this building were slight, of wattle and daub. Dr Rahtz suggested tentatively that it might be a central corn mill with a circular track for an animal or human labourer, and a grain store and bakery opening from it, but the interpretation is not a certain one. Immediately west of the hall was a small building with a pit, thought to be a latrine. Such was a late West Saxon royal hall, one of several which the kings owned, going from one to another in seasonal rotation.

An earlier king's residence was identified by Dr B. Hope-Taylor at Yeavering, Northumberland, 14 miles inland from the fortress of Bamborough. This was the *villa regalis* of Edwin of Northumbria, *Adgefrin*, where Paulinus taught and baptised in the early days of Christianity in the north. The complex was

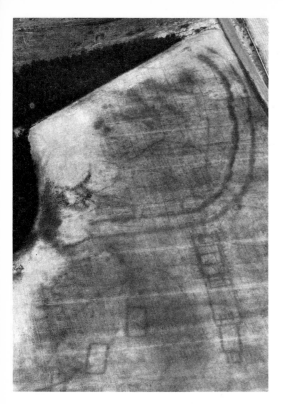
Crop-marks at Yeavering, showing the sites of buildings and of a defensive enclosure

not protected by artificial ramparts, but it included a large palisaded defensive enclosure suitable as a refuge, though this, being sixth century or earlier in its origin, antedated the Anglo-Saxon buildings. The latter are of the sixth and seventh centuries, and show a succession of occupations. Both enclosure and building sites yielded evidence that they were attacked by fire, presumably in warfare. The mid seventh century was a time of turmoil in Northumbria, for it saw the invasions and ravagings of Penda of Mercia, and the deaths in battle of the great kings Edwin and Oswald. Probably attack from this quarter destroyed Edwin's hall: like Hrothgar's in *Beowulf* it 'towered, tall and gabled, awaiting the tumult of battle, the hostile flame'. It was a timber building of squared posts set upright in a foundation trench and supported by buttresses. Internally, posts divided it into a central space with 'side-aisles', and one end was partitioned off as though for a private chamber. To the west of the hall was an unroofed bank of tiered seats in a wedge-shaped plan, and this seems to have been a meeting-place, whether for secular or religious purposes. Further west was a scatter of small, rectangular, timber buildings, one of which may have been a pagan temple converted later to Christian use. The picture given here is a simplified one, isolating one aspect of a site which was several times developed. The earliest buildings seem to have been of or before the reign of Aethelfrith, some probably dating from the second half of the sixth century. These Edwin replaced or adapted. When Edwin's *villa* was destroyed, Oswald built halls and outbuildings in a lighter structure, and added a church which gained an extensive cemetery. Even after the burning of Oswald's *villa* the site continued to be used, with rebuilt smaller halls and a new church.

More recently two further important manors have been found and partly published, those of Doon Hill, Dunbar, and Sulgrave, Northamptonshire, while work continues at Porchester Castle, Hampshire, where there are traces of a late aisled hall and yard. At Doon Hill two successive halls occupied a site within a polygonal palisaded enclosure. The first, which was pre-Anglo-Saxon, was destroyed by fire after 50–100 years of life, and an Anglo-Saxon building of the Yeavering type replaced it. Dr Hope-Taylor links these events to the Northumbrian thrust into Lothian in the reign of king Oswald. The Sulgrave hall was much later, from the eleventh century, and was a nobleman's seat, not a royal residence. Full details of the complex have not been published, but the main building was a timber-framed aisleless hall, 75 by 20 feet, part of the structure carried on stone footings. It had a dais at one end, a central hearth area, opposing doors in the long walls, and there may have been an upper floor.

For what it is worth, the Bayeux tapestry clinches some of the details given here in its schematic depictions of houses, detached gabled wooden (perhaps also stone) buildings with decorative

Edward the Confessor's palace

gable-posts and roofs of shingles or tiles. They are lit by round-headed windows, and have round-headed doorways with hinged doors strengthened with metal bands. Edward the Confessor's palace at Westminster seems to have defensive outbuildings, some detached from the main structure. Inside, it has textile hangings suspended from near the roof, and the king sits on a carved bench with embroidered cushion. Harold's palace apparently has a partly cobbled floor. Edward dies in an upper room, his bed surrounded by hangings which are looped round posts to keep them open, and Harold feasts also in an upper room at Bosham.

I have covered here a series of residences from widely different localities and dates. Clearly, they must have differed a lot in appearance, use and structural methods, too. Yet they have a good deal in common. A general pattern emerges of a group of buildings incorporating some element of defence, and a great hall, rectangular or nearly so and of timber, multi-purpose, lit and heated by a fire placed somewhere along the main axis.

We know much less of the homes of the great majority of the Anglo-Saxons, of the churls and the people beneath them in rank. The written sources do not describe them in any detail, nor had they been found, until very recently, in England. Alfred the Great introduced his translation of the *Soliloquies* with a picture of himself gathering wisdom as a man gathers timber in the forest: 'Then I collected sticks and props and shafts, and handles for all the tools I could use, and building wood and timbers, and, as far as I could carry them, the best beams for all the structures I could make. And I never brought one load home without wishing I could have fetched the whole wood if I could have carried it, for in each tree I saw something I needed at home. So I advise anyone who has the means and who has a lot of carts to make his way to the same wood where I cut these props, and to fetch himself more there, and to load his carts with well-shaped branches, so that he can interlace them to form neat walls, set up many splendid houses and build a fine dwelling. There he can live happily and comfortably in winter or summer as I have not yet been able to.'

I do not think that Alfred had any particular class of man clearly in mind when he wrote this, though he was certainly thinking of someone used to manual work. However, he gives us some idea, though only a faint one, of the Anglo-Saxon peasant's house. For detailed information, scholars have customarily relied on Continental Germanic material, notably that from Lower Saxony and south Jutland where conditions might resemble those of England. Important is a site of about 10,000 square metres at Warendorf, near Münster, Westphalia. This represents a short-lived settlement of the late seventh and eighth centuries. It held over 80 wooden buildings, pre-eminent among them being 11 barn-like long-houses, varying between 14 and 29 metres long, 4.5 and seven metres wide, the older ones rectangular in plan, the later examples boat-shaped, that is with bowed sides. At least six of these buildings had side-porches and hearths, and on this basis were considered to be dwellings. Others, without these features, were interpreted as workshops of some sort. Close to the long-houses and clearly dependent upon them economically were a number of small huts of a similar type, between four and 11 metres in length. Again, some had hearths and so were probably houses, others had none. There was also a scatter of rough sheds, some with sunken floors (*Grubenhäuser*, 'pit-dwellings'), but their function is not known. They may have been workshops, used for weaving, pottery-making, cooking or baking, but some at any rate may have been occupied or used for sleeping. A settlement of this design points to a class society, an upper one living in some luxury in the large long-houses, and a lower one in less state in the smaller huts while members of a depressed class may have occupied the *Grubenhäuser*. There is some resemblance here to an Anglo-Saxon society of free farmers, churls, served by a lower class and perhaps by slaves.

Perhaps the nearest approximation to Warendorf yet found in England is the Dark Age settlement at Maxey, Northamptonshire. The site is complex, and only about a third of it was recovered, so conclusions must be tentative. The excavator, Mr P. V. Addyman, thinks that there are here the buildings of a village (or just possibly, though less likely, an extensive single farm or manor), grouped in a haphazard way round a roughly rectangular open space, a wide street or a green. There were several largish barn-like structures of various sizes of the order 50 by 20 feet, 48 by 20 feet, 32 by 16 feet, set in different alignments. In the main the construction was of wooden posts, but the post-holes were not continuous and there were apparently planking or wattle-and-daub filling panels. Here and there were 'pit-dwellings', and there were also numbers of pits with stake-holes about them, suggesting small covered cellars for storage.

Elsewhere in England individual huts, not all certainly houses, have been excavated in quite large numbers. An eighth-century example at Sedgeford, Norfolk, was set on a hillside, drained by gulleys which carried away the surface water. It was 50 by *c.* 20 feet, had walls of wattle and daub, and a flint floor. A hut at Northolt, Middlesex, was only 15 by *c.* 18 feet. It had a small porch, a thick gravel floor and a hearth. Within the Roman defence wall at Dorchester on Thames was a

Reconstructions of buildings at Maxey

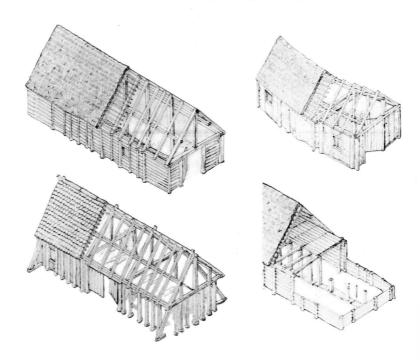

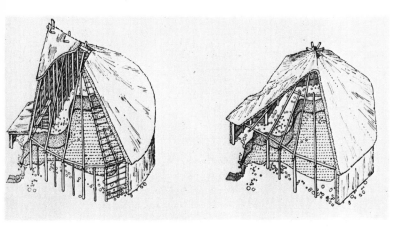

Suggested reconstructions of the Dorchester on Thames hut

building of the mid sixth century. Its plan was of irregular
shape, very roughly circular, about 16 feet across. The hut
floor was sunk to a level of about two feet six inches below the
surrounding earth, and had vertical sides round which the
stakes of the thinly covered wall were set. From the Roman
street a pavement of limestone flags led down a flight of three
stone steps into a narrow hall, and thence to the cleanly kept
floor, which at various times was of yellow loam, trampled
sandy earth and burnt red gravel. The periphery of the sunken
floor was marked by stake-holes which may have supported
seats or lockers. There was a hearth and perhaps a hollow
storage space for fuel. The roof must have been of light construction, with a louvre to let out the smoke. Equally comfort-
less must have been the shepherd's bothies, used only in spring
and summer, that St Cuthbert came upon near Chester-le-
Street. The roof of one was so low that his horse, reaching up,
could pull straw from it as fodder. If people lived much in huts
of this sort, it is not surprising that, as finds from some cemeteries have revealed, their leg-bones were abnormally worn with
over-much squatting.

Town houses are little known, for their sites have often been
continuously inhabited up to the present. Only recently has it
been possible to excavate deeply in such places as Canterbury,
Ipswich and Wareham, while Winchester and Thetford are
producing important results, as yet only partly published.
There is scattered written evidence too, but it is not clear how

147

we can combine our various bits of knowledge into a valid picture of Anglo-Saxon town life. What is true for Southampton may be false for York. Some towns, Canterbury and Rochester, for instance, were continuously occupied from very early times, but many others were developments of the later period, created to serve as markets, mint-places, strongholds and to some extent administrative centres. By modern standards all were small. It is impossible to give precise population statistics since we have only the Domesday assessments to go by, and those commissioners were not concerned with recording actual numbers of inhabitants. Moreover, some towns declined markedly in size between the end of the Anglo-Saxon period and the Domesday survey of 20 years later. The latest Domesday geographers give the following representative estimates for late Anglo-Saxon populations, though all are minimum figures, the real ones being higher but of the same order of magnitude. Large towns were Norwich, Lincoln and York, with over 5,000 inhabitants. Slightly smaller, over 4,000, were Thetford and Oxford. Dunwich, Huntingdon and Wallingford have 2,000–3,000, Canterbury about 2,500, Exeter, Leicester, Lewes and Nottingham in the region of 2,000, Chester about 1,500, Southampton 1,200, Hertford and Warwick 1,000, Stafford and Derby 750, St Albans and Malmesbury 500. London and Winchester do not appear in the Domesday Book.

Commonly a town was distinguished by its wall or rampart surrounding the settlement, as at Winchester where, in 1006, the citizens cowered at home watching 'an arrogant and fearless Viking host march past their gates to the sea, having fetched themselves supplies and treasures from more than 50 miles inland', and at York which the Vikings took in 867, and were shortly afterwards discomfited by a retaliatory English army 'for in those times that city had not as yet strong and stout walls'. Defences varied in type and quality. Sometimes they were incomplete, as apparently at Norwich, where excavation has so far failed to find a full encircling wall. Sometimes they were the old Roman ramparts repaired and secured, as at Winchester, Porchester and Carlisle. In the later towns built primarily for the defence of the realm, the kings must have employed skilled military architects, for the Anglo-Saxon defences are sometimes elaborate. At Lydford, Devon, the builders surrounded the town with a bank 40 feet wide. The site must have been marked out, and divided into sections which were constructed separately. The workmen then dug holes in the rock and stuck in upright timbers to give stability and perhaps to support fighting platforms. They laid parallel planks or beams on the ground, aligned at right angles to the bank axis. On these they put alternate layers of turfs and branches, finishing off with earth which they shaped into a steep front slope and a gentle back one. At Wallingford, Berkshire, Alfred's fortress had a rampart 35 feet wide. The builders stripped turf from the working area, dug a ditch and threw up the spoil of earth and gravel to form the bank. As this was unstable they laced it with vertical stakes rammed in as they were found necessary, while the turfs were used for a revetment at the back, and probably at the front, too.

Within a town's walled area the land was split into individual holdings, fenced off from one another; each was called a *haga*, 'hedged plot', or a *tun*, 'enclosure'. The later kings laid out their strongholds on royal estates. Within the ramparts the land was systematically marked out into properties to be let to the new inhabitants. Excavators have found traces of this at Lydford, where a sunken-floored hut, 34 by 14 feet, was built between parallel ditches, *c.* 85 feet apart, arranged at right-angles to the street system. At Thetford is an example of late Anglo-Saxon town planning. The settlement expanded rapidly in the tenth century. The inhabitants took over new land, and laid out the site with some attention to amenity and perhaps with some centralised control. The buildings were large and detached, spaciously set each in its own plot, bounded by small ditches. Across the site ran a metalled road, some 22 feet wide, with a narrower offshoot which led north to the Little Ouse. To the east was an industrial or artisans' quarter, with pottery kilns and metalworking. At Oxford there was a metalled road 20 feet broad, and houses built on to it in plots having an average frontage of about 25 feet, with open areas about 150 feet long at their backs, The older towns were less well organised.

In early Winchester the Anglo-Saxons built timber houses with floors cobbled with flints, stones and occasional animal bones over the Roman streets, which gave a firm and well-drained foundation. The early settlers at Mucking, Essex, built their squalid little town of some 60 huts over silted Roman ditches and at ditch intersections, showing that they retained the Roman field system. The huts are tiny 'pit-dwellings', 12 by 10 feet, with a floor of earth, mixed with charcoal and ash, a hearth and a deep post-hole at each end of the long axis. Some were workshops, for they yield lead waste and cast lead rings, and fired and unfired loom weights. At Canterbury the enclosed site became cramped, and there was development beyond the walls. Within them houses were closely packed. A ninth-century charter records the sale of a little plot of land by Ciolulf to Eanmund. The boundaries are listed: to the east Ethelmund the priest, to the south Deibearht, to the west Ciolulf, to the north Hemma. A somewhat later endorsement notes a customary law requiring two feet space between buildings as 'eavesdrip'.

The Anglo-Saxons had skilled builders in stone, as some of their church architecture testifies, and they also had a flourishing building-stone industry in the later period. They sometimes used this material for secular buildings, as we have seen at Sulgrave, as the Bayeux tapestry suggests, and as Alfred's biographer, bishop Asser, describes. Perhaps they worked in brick, too. Yet most domestic buildings were of wood. With their open hearths, roofs low and often thatched, and their sometimes slight wooden walls, they must have been very susceptible to fire. The Dorchester on Thames hut, for instance, perished in this way, and Bede's graphic account of a miracle attributed to St Oswald shows how easily a cottage could go up in flames. A British traveller, passing the spot where the saint-king died in battle, took up some of the earth and bound it in a linen cloth. Going his way, he came to a village where someone was holding a party. He was invited to join it, so he went into the house, hanging his cloth on a beam. 'They sat feasting and drinking for a good time, with a blazing fire in the middle of the room, when sparks flew up and caught the house roof, which, being of wattle covered with thatch, quickly burst into flames. When the fuddled party-goers spotted this, they rushed in terror out of the house, incapable of putting out the blaze . . . so that the house burned down.' Only the beam bearing the cloth with the earth sanctified by Oswald's martyr-death escaped. If houses were closely packed the danger of destruction of a whole settlement was high, and indeed there were disastrous fires at York in 741 and at Canterbury in 756. A corollary is that a saint's virtue could be proved by his ability to avert such disaster, as St Cuthbert did when the wind changed direction at his prayers, or St Aidan when, from the distant Farne Islands, he saw the enemy's flames rising against the town of Bamborough, and drove them back upon their kindlers by his exclamation of horror.

No Anglo-Saxon house furniture has survived, nor are there detailed descriptions of it, while contemporary drawings of such things as chairs and beds are of doubtful accuracy. I have already indicated some of the furnishings of the hall—the built-in benches, wall-hangings, seat-coverings, mattress beds and trestle tables—while the remaining traces of smaller huts often suggest that they too had built-in seat-beds and storage lockers. The wills, particularly those of women, mention chests (sometimes specified as used for clothes or spinning materials), 'a good cabinet, well decorated', bed-clothing, curtains and linen coverings, as well as a table-cover. The laws expect the woman of a household to have a coffer which could be locked as a safe deposit. The obscure Exeter Riddle 49, which describes an object 'standing fixed to the ground' which 'often during the day swallows useful gifts from a servant's hand', may have as answer 'a book-chest'.

Of the table-ware we know more. Wills and other official documents often refer to cups, goblets and drinking-horns. The metal fittings of horns survive from such sites as Taplow, Trewhiddle, Cornwall and Sutton Hoo, often of great beauty. Seven horns were found at Sutton Hoo, five of them forming a set made from cows' horn. The other two were a huge pair—in reconstructed form one holds six quarts—of the now extinct aurochs horn. Wynflaed bequeathed 'her two *wesendhornas*', which were probably also aurochs. Exeter Riddle 14 describes a fine drinking-horn: 'Sometimes, adorned with decorations, I hang splendidly on the wall where men are drinking'. Sutton Hoo has also a pottery bottle, cups made from gourds, and some silver spoons, dishes and a ladle imported from the east. Cuthbert, abbot of Wearmouth, asked Lull of Mainz to send him 'any man in your diocese who can make glass vessels well . . . because we are ignorant and destitute of that art', yet there are a surprising number of Anglo-Saxon glasses, some made in England, some imported from the Continent. They are of various shapes, jars, cups, claw- and cone-beakers, bottles and even drinking horns. All these were presumably the property only of the rich. The poor made do with wood or pottery. The metal mounts of bronze-bound wooden buckets are quite common finds, and the 'six tubs, two buckets, three trenchers (*trog*)' listed in a catalogue of Peterborough property at Yaxley, Huntingdonshire, were presumably also wooden. The wealthy Wynflaed left a gold-decorated wooden cup, and two others 'ornamented with dots'. The turned wooden bowl from Hungate, York, had split in two, and was precious enough

Drinking horns from Sutton Hoo

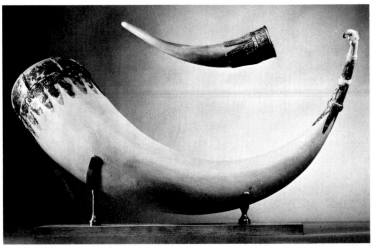

*Anglo-Saxon
glassware*

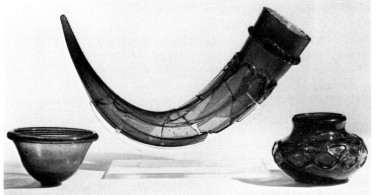

to be repaired with metal rivets. For everyday use and for common work there was coarse pottery, which survives in huge quantities from sites of all dates and types: cooking pots, pitchers, water-bottles, bowls and large storage jars.

Further Reading

There is no up-to-date account of Anglo-Saxon houses in general, for only now are their sites being discovered in large numbers. Readers should keep an eye on the yearly reports in *Medieval Archaeology* which are often the first printed accounts of new finds. The same journal gives detailed excavation reports and general summaries of material, as C. A. R. Radford, 'The Saxon House: a Review and Some Parallels' (vol. I), P. A. Rahtz, 'The Saxon and Medieval Palaces at Cheddar, Somerset' (vol. VI–VII), and P. V. Addyman, K. R. Fennell and L. Biek, 'A Dark-Age Settlement at Maxey, Northants,' (vol. VIII), and there are also descriptions of the examinations of Anglo-Saxon burghal defences. For the sizes of town populations in the late Anglo-Saxon period, see the various Domesday Geographies, edited by H. C. Darby.

X

Vanities

The Rhyming Poem portrays the happy patrician, surrounded by the world's delights. Some of these are the privileges of rank: power of command over servants, control of an army, a ship or an estate, the enjoyment of being generous to loyal retainers. Some are the common human joys: friendship, good company, the world of nature. Some are the pleasures which Anglo-Saxon man allowed himself: the feast, riding the swift horse, the harp struck in the hall, the splendour of apparel. Such pleasures the Anglo-Saxon moralists were moved to attack, especially when life's difficulties led them to believe that God was taking revenge upon a luxurious and vicious people. After the Vikings sacked Lindisfarne in 793, Alcuin warned the survivors against feasting ('let your banquets be in soberness, not in drunkenness') and love of dress ('empty adornment of clothing and useless elegance is a reproach before men and a sin before God'). Writing to Aethelred of Northumbria on the same occasion Alcuin listed the sins the English were committing, but also rebuked their vanities, 'the luxurious habits of princes and people'; 'the immoderate use of clothing'; 'delicacies and feastings'. Earlier, Bede had urged archbishop Ecgbert of York to reform the church, and to correct prelates given to 'laughter, jests, tales, feasting and drunkenness'. Among the decrees of the 747 Council of *Clofeshoh* was one forbidding sports and horse-racing on Rogation Days, which must be kept for holy exercises. Naturally, those whose eyes were fixed on a higher world had little time for the vanities of this; but most Anglo-Saxons persisted in their bad habits.

Feasting was the pleasure of the rich and the solace of the

poor. The *Rectitudines* tells of the common right of workmen to a harvest feast for reaping the corn, and a drinking feast for ploughing. Aelfric deplores the custom of holding drinking parties at dead men's wakes, and toping over the body. Penitentials suggest that the pagan English held sacrificial feasts which may have continued in the festivals of Christian times. Such were the celebrations of the common run of men, but in the literature, of course, it is the banquets of the kings and noblemen which get most attention. Bede tells of the saintly Oswald's compassion on the poor beggars at his gate when he was holding an Easter feast. So distressed was he at their misery that he gave them both the rich foods before him and the silver dish they were served on. An early *Life of St Dunstan* relates the disgraceful behaviour of king Eadwig, who left his coronation banquet to frolic with his mistresses, and had to be dragged by force to rejoin the waiting nobles.

In Anglo-Saxon poetry the aristocratic life is epitomised by the 'joys of life in the hall'. This is how the protagonist of *The Wanderer*, in his exile, remembers the courtly life, 'the retainers in hall, the receipt of treasure, how in his youth his generous lord regaled him at the feast'. *The Runic Poem* speaks of the 'sport and laughter among proud men, where warriors sit

'The joys of life in the hall'

blithely together in the beer-hall'. Symbolising the good life, *The Rhyming Poem* says simply, 'feasts never failed'. *Beowulf* describes in detail several of these occasions, stressing the drinking —of mead, wine or beer—rather than the eating. After Grendel's defeat, the hall Heorot is decorated, the walls covered with golden hangings. Men take their places at the benches round their king, and drink many a cup of mead. The king presents gifts to Beowulf and his companions, and orders due compensation to be paid for a man whom Grendel has slain. The court minstrel plays and sings. The cupbearers serve wine. The queen comes forward and offers the cup to the king and the guests. When the party comes to an end, the men clear away the benches and lay out their beds for sleep. Clearly there was a formal side to feasting. The after-dinner speeches which *Beowulf* records may have been common practice. Other sources show the woman of the house at her office of serving the cup to the master and the chief guests: 'At the banquet she shall always, everywhere, before the band of comrades greet the protector of warriors first of all, quickly offer the first cup to her lord's hand.' Apparently a king or noble's retainers were expected at a mead-drinking to make promises or boasts about their loyalty to their lord, boasts they must fulfil on the battlefield. After Byrhtnoth's death in the battle of Maldon, one of his men, Aelfwine, urges his fellows to 'remember the speeches we often made over the mead, when we warriors in hall raised our boasts at the bench about harsh battle. Now we can test who is brave'. The author of *The Fight at Finnesburh* tells how king Hnaef's warriors kept their word, for he had never heard of a band of men who repaid the bright mead which their lord gave them better than these did.

There was also an informal side to feasting. Too often it seems to have degenerated into drunkenness and confusion, for Anglo-Saxon literature is full of warnings against the brawls which may arise. In *The Fates of Men* 'an angry drinker, a man sodden with wine' is cut down at the bench because he has been 'too hasty in his words'. *A Warning against Pride* shows what happens 'when wine whets a warrior's spirit, and tumult and outcry break out in the company'. By the laws of Hlothhere and Eadric anyone who drew a weapon in a house where men were drinking had to pay heavy fines, even if he did no injury. From the time of Tacitus the Germanic peoples had been renowned for their drinking bouts. The Anglo-Saxons carried on the tradition, and even their clergy were notorious for it. St Aethelwold of Winchester himself seems to have encouraged drinking, if Aelfric's biography is to be believed. King Eadred, his retinue and some Northumbrian guests, were invited to dine at the monastery of Abingdon, then under the saint's charge. The king ordered a good supply of mead, and had the doors locked so that nobody could leave. Though they drank heavily all day, the supply of mead hardly decreased, and the story ends with the Northumbrians 'swinishly intoxicated.' On a more modest level Boniface wrote to Ecgbert of York, asking for advice and sending 'two little casks of wine, because we love each other; do enjoy them with your brethren'.

Accompaniment to the feast was the harp, the most frequently mentioned Anglo-Saxon instrument. *The Rhyming Poem* describes its sound: 'The harp was resonant, it rang out loudly. Its voice re-echoed, the lilt of the music was melodious', and there are common periphrases for the instrument, as *gomenwudu*, 'wood of delight', *gleobeam*, 'pleasure-beam'. *The Fates of Men* gives some idea how it was played: 'One man shall sit with his harp at his lord's feet and gain wealth, plucking the strings rapidly, making the leaping plectrum, the ringing nail, sound forth.' The minstrel used it, we are told, to accompany his singing, presumably to mark the time scheme of his verse and to add ornamentation. *Beowulf* shows us the celebrations following the opening of the great hall Heorot: 'There was the sound of the harp, the clear song of the minstrel.' After Beowulf had driven out Grendel, 'there was song and music together before Healfdene's battle-leader [king Hrothgar]. The harp was struck, the tale often told, when, as became his office, Hrothgar's minstrel declaimed among the mead-benches of the hall.' Harping was a gentleman's accomplishment. Returning home, Beowulf describes how the old king of the Danes entertained him after the battle with the monstrous Grendel. 'There was song and mirth. The old Scylding [Dane], who had heard tell many things, spoke of far-off times. Now and again that brave warrior touched the wood of delight, the harp's joy; at times he told stories, true and sad; at times the great-hearted king related strange tales.' The same aristocratic background appears in *Widsith*. The journeying minstrel who is the poem's hero boasts that 'when with clear voice Scilling [? the harp's name, ? the name of an accompanying singer] and I raised our song before our victorious lord—the voice made loud melody to the harp—then many bold men, who knew what they were talking about, said that they had never heard a better song.' Significant, too, are the finds of three small harps or lyres in very rich burials, at Sutton Hoo, Abingdon and Taplow. All are fragmentary, but enough remains of the Sutton Hoo specimen to suggest a reconstruction. The latest research shows it as a round lyre, about thirty inches tall and eight wide. The body is of maple wood partly hollowed out to give resonance, with tuning pegs of willow or poplar, and six strings which were probably of gut or horse-hair.

A king (in this case David) harping

The harp was not an upper-class instrument only, for it is unlikely that the instrumentalists who gave names to Harperley, Durham, or Harper's Brook, Northampton, were aristocrats. Bede's story of the divine inspiration granted to the cattleman Caedmon at Whitby shows the working class in relaxation. Caedmon had never learned to sing, 'and so it sometimes happened at a party, when for merriment's sake they resolved that everybody should sing in turn, if he saw the harp coming in his direction he would get up from the feast, go out and return home'. On one of these occasions he went to sleep in the shippon, dreamt that an angel ordered him to sing of the creation of the world, and woke up a minstrel. The harp mentioned here was clearly a small hand-harp which could be passed round and played by each reveller where he sat. It seems it was fairly unusual for a man not to be able to attempt a song, for Caedmon was ashamed of his incompetence.

The clergy too accepted the harp. It was after all a biblical instrument, and Anglo-Saxon illustrations to the Psalter show David accompanying his songs on the hand-harp, usually the triangular *cythara anglica*. St Dunstan was a skilled performer, using a harp small enough to be hung on the wall when it was not in use. Cuthbert of Wearmouth, as we have seen, begged Lull of Mainz to send him a harper if he could find one, yet he seems to have been uneasy at asking: 'I pray you will not scorn my request nor think it laughable.' He may have felt his desire too worldly, the harp too closely linked with secular poetry. Certainly this is how Alcuin thought of it when, at the end of the eighth century, he wrote to bishop Higbald of Lindisfarne warning him: 'Let God's words be read in the refectory. There it is proper to listen to a lector, not a harpist; to the sermons of the fathers, not the songs of the heathens. For what has Ingeld [one of the heroes of vernacular poetry] to do with Christ? Our house is narrow. It won't be able to hold both.'

We know little about other musical instruments of the Anglo-Saxons. Exeter Riddle 31 is thought to describe a type of bagpipe: 'Its nose pointed downwards, its feet and hands like a bird . . . yet it has in its foot beautiful music, the delightful gift of song.' It is played indoors at feasts, and passed round from hand to hand. The answer to Riddle 69 may be 'a shepherd's pipe'. 'It sings through its sides, and has a crooked neck, skilfully made. It has two sharp shoulders . . . and it stands by the wayside.' Prince Athelstan's will bequeathes to his brother Edmund 'a silver-coated trumpet'; Old English *bymere*, 'trumpeter', occurs in the place-name Bemerton, Wiltshire;

and Old English *hornblawere*, 'hornblower', in Hornblotton, Somerset. Presumably trumpet and horn were not musical instruments proper, but usually served to summon men to battle or to banquet, as the Exeter Riddle 14 describes and the Bayeux tapestry depicts. The mid-eleventh-century manuscript, Cotton Tiberius c vi, whose iconography is Anglo-Saxon, shows David harping, accompanied by a hornblower, a man with a long pipe and another playing the rebec. A fourth man juggles with three knives and three balls, and is clearly related to a similar figure on Trinity College, Cambridge, ms b.5.26, who can manipulate three knives only. There may have been many such entertainers, the type of men *The Endowments of Men* describes as 'very active, lithe and supple, having tricks of skill, the gift of amusing pranks before men'.

Most medieval literature survives only by happy chance. A lot of Anglo-Saxon material was oral and popular, and the clerics responsible for preserving most of our texts thought it unworthy of writing down, or not worth wasting parchment on. Occasionally a work of pure entertainment remains, such as the fragmentary lay *The Fight at Finnesburh* which describes how 60 warriors defended a hall valiantly against superior force, or the romantic prose tale *Apollonius of Tyre*, a story of wicked kings and courtiers, storm and shipwreck, kidnapping, long-lost children dramatically rediscovered, and true love triumphant at the end. But these are rare, and we usually have only descriptions of what was sung or told for diversion. William of Malmesbury relates how St Aldhelm used to attract a reluctant audience to his sermons. Noticing his congregation thin out as soon as mass was complete, Aldhelm took his stand on the bridge they had to cross to get home, 'like a man professing the art of singing'. The people stopped to hear his merry songs, but as soon as he had got his audience, he changed his act by adding scriptural material, and so painlessly edified his flock. Asser recalls how the young Alfred could not read, yet he 'listened attentively to Saxon poems day and night, and hearing them often recited by others committed them to his retentive memory'. Even in later life Alfred learned vernacular poems by heart, and encouraged others to do so too. There may also have been an oral prose tradition. Histories and saints' lives from Anglo-Saxon England are full of comments implying that story-telling was common, either as reports by partakers or eye-witnesses of events, or tales passed down from man to man. For example, Bede's *Life of St Cuthbert* relates how the holy man's prayers saved a number of monks on timber-carrying rafts from being blown out to sea, while a group of jeering landsmen looked on. The monk who informed Bede 'said he had often heard one of that very group, a simple peasant, incapable of lying, tell the tale before a large audience'. The sword-bearer who accompanied St Edmund of East Anglia to his last battle later told king Athelstan how the king had died. Dunstan, then a young man, was present; in old age he recounted the incidents to Abbo of Fleury who used it for his *Passio sancti Eadmundi*. Asser tells the story of the wicked Eadburh to explain why the wife of the West Saxon king did not receive the title of queen. This he got from Alfred who must have heard it from his elders, since it referred to events about a century earlier. This sort of evidence suggests there may have been a tradition of saga-telling, both for edification and entertainment, such as existed in medieval Iceland. No original examples survive, save perhaps for the story of Cyneheard and Cynewulf's struggle for the West Saxon throne, preserved in the 755 *Chronicle* and distinguished from the exiguous surrounding entries by its vividness and detail.

Perhaps the vernacular verse riddles, about 100 of which survive, formed a traditional part of indoor amusement. Many of them are clearly learned, and must be seen as conscious copies of the Latin riddle tradition, perhaps composed as formal exercises and certainly within educated communities. But others may have been meant as oral puzzles—one challenges *werum æt wine*, 'men over their wine', to guess the answer —and the indelicate, insinuating or plain bawdy descriptions of some extant examples suggest a rather coarser audience than that of the schools, and one seeking a simple if rude amusement.

The Anglo-Saxons also passed the time with dice and board games, though details of them are sparse and the surviving vocabulary is imprecise or inadequately understood. Tacitus describes the Germani as compulsive gamblers and lot-casters, and some of this the Anglo-Saxons inherited. The word *tæfl*, which glosses Latin *alea*, is used for a board game played with dice, perhaps for other board games, and possibly for the dice themselves. *The Fates of Men* refers to those who have 'skill at *tæfl*, the trick of the coloured board', apparently some game played on a parti-coloured board like that of modern chequers, and this would fit the more general reference in the Exeter gnomic verses, 'two shall sit at *tæfl* until their sorrow glides away from them; they forget harsh fate and enjoy themselves

Chessman from Witchampton Manor

at the table'. No such gaming board has survived from Anglo-Saxon England though there are early continental specimens and a Viking example, probably made in the Isle of Man in the tenth century, with 49 peg-holes instead of squares, set seven by seven, the central hole marked by concentric circles. Common in graves are sets of playing-pieces, usually domed discs of bone, often decorated with incised circles. They abound in cremation burials in East Anglia, and also occur in seventh-century inhumations as at Taplow, Buckinghamshire, and Sarre and Faversham, Kent. An urn at Caistor-by-Norwich contained 33 pieces, about a third of them black, of ivory, and two-thirds white, of bone. Keythorpe Hall, Tugby, Lincolnshire, had a set of 46 discs, with a pair of dice and a semi-globular object which may have been a special piece. From Haslingfield, Cambridgeshire, and Castle Bytham, Lincolnshire, are horse's teeth, rubbed or ground down at the bases and with tops carved or shaped, and these may be board-game pieces. From the Scandinavian evidence, and that of a game drawn in an eleventh-century gospel-book in an Irish hand, it looks as though the Anglo-Saxons played a game in which one side, small in number but with a king, occupied the centre of a chequered board, while a larger one took the outer edges. The pieces may have been moved to the throw of a dice. The smaller

*Rune-inscribed astragalus
from Caistor-by-Norwich*

side tried to clear a way for their king to the board edge, while the larger side attempted to hem in the king so that it could not move.

Also found in early graves are sets of sheep's *astragali*, ankle-bones conveniently shaped for playing-pieces since they are roughly cubic. These could have served some game similar to our knuckle-bones or jacks. Caistor-by-Norwich again produced a set, much damaged by the cremation fire. There were at least 31 of these bones, the largest and darkest having a mysterious inscription which runologists have not yet deciphered. Finds of dice show that this simple form of gambling was frequent. Cnut may have known chess, though there is no evidence that the game was generally played in England before the Norman Conquest.

Outdoor amusements listed in *The Endowments of Men* are horse riding and management, swimming, running and archery, and to these we may speculatively add other sports which trained the young for the rigours of warfare. Hunting was popular, and there must have been games and pastimes such as the sword-dancing which Tacitus describes, or the primitive and rough ball-games known in medieval Scandinavia. Old English had such words as *plegstow* and *plegestede*, 'sports-ground', and these survive in numbers of place-names like Plaistow, Plaxtol, Plestowes and notably in field-names, while a related *plegsteall* occurs in Chapel Plaster, Wiltshire.

The Anglo-Saxons enjoyed handling and racing horses. One of the pleasures stressed in *The Rhyming Poem* is the horse, gay in its trappings, which carried the young nobleman 'with long strides delightfully across the plains'. *The Runic Poem* defines *eh*, 'stallion, horse', as 'the joy of princes' and 'the solace of the restless'. *Beowulf* shows the courtiers, on the way back from the mere where Grendel took refuge, racing their mounts wherever the paths look sound. Among other miracles, John of Beverley cured by his prayers and ministrations a young man who had fallen from his horse and broken his skull. Against the bishop's express command he had joined in an impromptu contest which a group of the bishop's companions, 'mainly

Hawk, horse and hound

layfolk', had got up when they found themselves on 'a level open way, suited for racing horses'. In the Scandinavian parts of the country place-names record horse-racing, and also apparently horse-fighting of a Scandinavian type—two stallions were set face to face, and goaded on by their owners to fight one another with teeth and hoofs. Hesket, Cumberland, and Hesketh, Yorkshire and Lancashire, derive from Old Norse *hestaskeith*, 'race-track for horses'; Follifoot and Follithwaite, Yorkshire, seem to be Old English *folagefeoht*, 'horse-fight'; and Rosewain, Cumberland, may be *hrossgewinn*, which has the same sense. Anglo-Saxon wills often dispose of large numbers of horses—that of Wulfgeat leaves to his lord two horses, 10 mares and 10 colts, to one Brun six mares with six colts, and an un-numbered remainder to be divided equally among his wife and daughters. Prince Athelstan's will catalogues his horses with care: the one he had from Thurbrand, and the white horse that Leofwine gave him were to go to his father, king Aethelred, a black stallion to bishop Aelfsige, a horse with harness to his chaplain Aelfwine, a pied stallion to the seneschal Aelfmaer, a horse to Siferth, and a whole stud to the staghuntsman. Elaborate horse-trappings—copper-inlaid stirrup irons, for example—survive to show the Anglo-Saxon noble's affection for and pride in his steed.

Asser speaks of Alfred's care that the young men of his court should receive formal education before they were ready for 'hunting and other pursuits which are fitting for noblemen'.

Wolf-hunting

An elaborately inlaid stirrup iron

Hunting and falconry were indeed popular among the upper classes and some of the examples in chapter VI should properly belong here. Alfred practised every branch of hunting, and even dared to instruct his falconers, hawkers and kennelmen. Aethelberht II of Kent wrote to Boniface in Germany, asking him to send a pair of falcons capable of bringing down cranes, since Kent could produce nothing suitable. The opening of *The Battle of Maldon* shows the English troops drawn up in battle array, with one of the young fighters, unnamed but seemingly of good family, amusing himself—or showing coolness in the face of the enemy—by hawking. He soon found that his general, Byrhtnoth, 'would not tolerate slackness', so he released his hawk to the neighbouring copse before advancing to his position. Even the clergy seem to have enjoyed blood-sports, for we find Alcuin warning the monks of Wearmouth and Jarrow not to allow young men under their supervision to dig foxes from their earths or to course hares. He adds sourly, 'How wicked to leave the service of Christ for a fox-hunt!'

Of other manly sports we hear little. As a youth Beowulf took part in a foolhardy swimming match with a comrade, Breca, and after several days in the sea, harassed by monsters, landed up at ?Finnheden, Småland. A place-name like Bathley, Nottinghamshire, meaning 'clearing where there are bathing places', seems to point to a place in the Trent where there was swimming for sport. The Bayeux tapestry shows a man fighting a tied bear. One of Aelfric's homilies tells of the sad but wholesome fate of a fool who persisted in drinking during Lent: after one such draught he walked outside and was promptly gored by a bull that was being baited there.

'The princes' superfluity is the people's poverty', thundered Alcuin, indicting the luxury of dress that some of the rich main-

Bear-baiting

tained. The complaint is a common one right through the Middle Ages. Unfortunately, practically nothing survives of Anglo-Saxon clothing to support the accusation, and from drawings it is hard to discern the luxury of exotic stuffs or fashions. The pictures of Athelstan presenting his book to St Cuthbert (Corpus Christi College, Cambridge, MS 183), of Edgar at the refounding of New Minster, Winchester (Cotton Vespasian A viii), and of Cnut in the New Minster *Liber Vitae* (British Museum Stowe MS 944) show no startling dressiness. The kings are sensibly and warmly clad in long-sleeved knee-length tunics gathered in at the waist, mantles fastened at one shoulder, hose or leggings and light shoes. The only signs of excess are embroidered hems and cuffs, elaborate brooches holding the mantles, with perhaps fur trimmings to Edgar's. Queen Aelfgifu, who accompanies Cnut, has a simple long gown and mantle, a close-fitting headdress flowing into decorative lappets at the back, and an ornamented headband. The pictures agree adequately with Aldhelm's description of Anglo-Saxon dress at the end of the seventh century, when he was complaining of the worldliness of some religious attire: 'In both sexes this kind of costume consists of a fine linen undergarment, a red or blue tunic, a headdress and sleeves with silk borders; their shoes are covered with red dyed leather; . . . instead of head coverings they wear white and coloured veils which hang down luxuriantly to the feet and are held in place by headbands sewn on to them.' It seems that to the Anglo-Saxon luxury lay in using more delicate materials than were usual, finely spun and woven wool and linen with occasional silk, in having the stuff dyed rather than plain, and in trimming the garments with embroidery and fine jewellery. Relevant here is Mrs S. C. Hawkes's study of fragments of

Entertainers

167

Reconstruction of gold-threaded braid from Taplow

elaborate gold-brocaded tablet-woven bands from early graves, mainly in south-east England. The seventh-century chieftain of Taplow, Buckinghamshire, was buried in his clothing, but all that remains are some pieces of gold-threaded woollen braid, probably parts of a tunic border, and of a belt and baldric which were further adorned with a gold buckle and gilt clasps. There are similar fragments from rich women's graves, where they seem to represent gold headbands or bracelets. Valuable bands like these are disposed of in some of the wills. For example, Wulfwaru's describes two, one of 30 mancuses (=900 pennies), and one of 20, while the joint will of Brihtric and Aelfswith mentions one which was valuable enough to be cut in two, half to be given to Rochester cathedral and half to St Augustine's, Canterbury. Other pieces of clothing were sometimes important enough to appear in wills: fur gowns (*crusne*), cloaks (*hakele*), robes (*pell*—the word implies costly material). Wynflaed's will catalogues several articles of dress, tunics (*tunece*), gowns (*cyrtel*), mantles (*mentel*), caps (*cuffie*), headbands, some defined by technical adjectives whose meanings we do not know.

The comparative coarseness and simplicity of the cloth must have set off the glitter and delicacy of texture of much of the jewellery the rich Anglo-Saxon delighted in. Before buttons or hooks and eyes were thought of, the brooch served the purpose of clasping the garments together. Anglo-Saxon brooches survive in great numbers, and in an immense variety of shapes and materials. There are disc, penannular and ring brooches; bow brooches which may be equal-armed, cruciform, long or square-headed; brooches shaped as trefoils, or like birds or animals. They may be of bronze, which could be gilded, or silver or gold, decorated with chip-carving or filigree, with *cloisonné* garnets or coloured glass, with shell, with niello or enamel. They vary a lot in quality, elaboration and taste. The most impressive use combinations of materials and techni-

168

ques; such pieces as the Kingston, Kirkoswald, Dowgate Hill and Fuller brooches must have been very costly. Other accessories, such as strap-ends, buckles, pins and wrist clasps, were often highly ornamented, and the jeweller also made rings, pendants and necklaces. Women wore long strings of multi-coloured beads, suspended across the breast, or as girdles. Men had a further means of

Gold and garnet pendant from Faversham

adornment in the weapons they carried, for these were sometimes richly decorated. Here again archaeological and written evidence combine, for the wills are once more informative. Ealdorman Aelfheah's mentions a short sword on whose scabbard (*lecg*) there are 80 mancuses of gold, while Aelfgar left a 'sword which king Edmund gave me, which was worth 120 mancuses of gold and had four pounds of silver on the sheath'. Prince Athelstan bequeathed several swords, three with silver hilts. Three surviving specimens, chosen from many, illustrate some of this splendour. The Sutton Hoo sword has a gold pommel set with garnets, filigree gold mounts on the hilt, and a scabbard with gold and garnet bosses, all of the finest workmanship. From Fetter Lane, London, comes an early ninth-century pommel and sword-grip of silver, parcel gilt. It has delicately carved decoration of swirling snakes, a conventional animal, and leaf, tendril and scroll patterns, the design thrown up by a background of niello. The blade of a scramasax, or short one-edged sword, from the Thames at Battersea is of iron, inlaid with copper, bronze and silver. These form patterns of straight and zigzag lines and of dots, as well as giving the runic alphabet and the name Beagnoth, also in runes.

Pommel and sword-grip from Fetter Lane, London

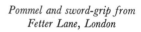

Such weapons must have represented a big capital investment. Aelfgar valued his sword at 120 mancuses, that is 3,600 pence. The sheath had four pounds of silver: 960 pence at the rate of 240 to the pound—if that is the correct rate in this case. An ox was worth 30 pence, a slave one pound. The difference in standard of living between a nobleman who could afford such treasures and a poor freeman or slave must have been immense. The rich man of *The Rhyming Poem* boasts, 'I was bold in array, noble in equipment. My pleasure was lordly, my life joyful.' For the wealthy it could be a good life. But one does not have to be a socialist or a puritan to respond to Alcuin's appeal to Aethelred of Northumbria: 'Some labour under an enormity of clothes, others perish with cold. Some are inundated with delicacies and feasts like Dives clothed in purple, and Lazarus dies of hunger at the gate. Where is brotherly love? Where the pity which we are admonished to have for the wretched? The satiety of the rich is the hunger of the poor. . . . Be rulers of the people, not robbers; shepherds, not plunderers.'

Further Reading

There is no single book covering all the material of this chapter, though individual works deal with parts of it. For the harp, and its use in accompanying verse, J. C. Pope, *The Rhythm of Beowulf*, 2nd ed., 1966, pp. 88–95. The new construction of the Sutton Hoo musical instrument will shortly be published by R. L. S. Bruce-Mitford. I wish to thank him for allowing me to publish details of it before the official account. C. E. Wright illustrates the oral tradition of literature in *The Cultivation of Saga in Anglo-Saxon England*. Some aspects of luxurious dress are described in E. Crowfoot and S. C. Hawkes, 'Early Anglo-Saxon Gold Braids', *Medieval Archaeology*, vol. XI, 1967. R. F. Jessup, *Anglo-Saxon Jewellery*, shows a splendid selection of fine jewels.

Scramasax from the river Thames at Battersea

Index

Numerals in **bold type** indicate pages on which illustrations appear